The Spirit of Cooking

The Spirit of Cooking

BEHIND THE SCENES

WITH NORTHERN CALIFORNIA'S BEST CHEFS

BY
SID GOLDSTEIN

Published by:

LAND OF PLENTY
PRODUCTIONS

787 22nd Ave.
San Francisco, CA 94121
Produced in cooperation with Grgich Hills Cellar, Rutherford, CA.

THE SPIRIT OF COOKING
BEHIND THE SCENES
WITH NORTHERN CALIFORNIA'S BEST CHEFS

BY
SID GOLDSTEIN

Published by:
Land of Plenty Productions
787 22nd Ave.
San Francisco, CA 94121

Copyright © 1984 by Sid Goldstein
First Printing: 1984
Printed in the United States

Art Director: Jeffrey Caldewey
Cover Design & Book Layout: Ronna Nelson
Edited by: Leslie Harlib & Suzanne Goldstein
Color Separations: Great Western Graphics,
          Commerce City, CO
Printed by: BookCrafters, Inc., Chelsea, MI
Typesetting: Typographics, St. Helena, CA
Logo: Dan Reich
Library of Congress Catalog Card #: 84-48114
          ISBN: 0-917887-01-8

All photographs by Sid Goldstein
Front Cover: Chef John Canepa at Tadich Grill fires up a sauté pan.

DEDICATION

This book is dedicated to Suzanne, whose encouragement, faith, and love helped me through this project; to Zachary, who has opened my eyes in wonderment; and to my mother, Lois, who taught me that food is more than something you put in your mouth because you are hungry.

ACKNOWLEDGEMENTS

This book would not have been possible without the assistance of the chefs and restaurants who are included. Special thanks are also in order to Jeffrey Caldewey, Ronna Nelson, Leslie Harlib, Austin Hills, Mike Grgich, Susan Atkin, Joanne Donsky, Barry Bone, and Linda Frazier.

CONTENTS

CONTENTS

APPENDIX

San Francisco is arguably the world's finest food city. In terms of its ethnic influences and diversification of cuisine, its top chefs of varied backgrounds from around the world, the quality of fresh, local ingredients, its connection to the wine industry and its serious, eating public, there are not many places which can compare. Yes, Paris may offer the ultimate in elegant dining; New York has extraordinary restaurants of all origins; Hong Kong, Bangkok, Singapore and Tokyo all excel in their own cooking traditions, but San Francisco (the Bay Area and Northern California) has it all.

The facts alone speak for themselves: San Francisco itself has some 4300 restaurants (92 per square mile or one for every 164 residents), according to a 1983 survey. The restaurant business is estimated to be the city's largest industry, annually grossing some $870 million. San Franciscans love to eat out and have since the mid-1800's when the Gold Rush brought hungry and often wealthy miners to our fabled city looking for good times.

Dining is glamorous; cooking is not. It is precisely this notion which inspired me to write this book. As I sat on a sunny patio at Chico's Paradise, outside Puerto Vallarta, in 1983 and watched an old Mexican woman pound out tortillas in an open kitchen, it occured to me that the real "spirit of cooking" goes on behind-the-scenes, and that we, as diners, only experience the final result of all the labor, creativity and hard work.

As with theater, there is a certain mystique about what happens in the kitchen before "the curtain goes up" and our senses are dazzled by the performance which follows. And so this book will attempt to uncover and reveal elements of that mystique, mostly in the words of the chefs themselves and with photographs and recipes which hopefully capture the essence of the chef.

The culinary scene in Northern California is as much a "melting pot" as the area itself. The chefs represent an amalgamation of traditional and modern philosophies. With the more traditional chefs, the emphasis is on retaining the essence of the natural food product itself with simple preparation and presentation. This type of cooking relates, more or less, to good home cooking where the palate and soul are nourished through a direct relationship between the food, the chef, and the eater with few distractions.

Cooking is very much tradition and experience, as much as it is vision and creativity. While change and experimentation can be exciting and rewarding, the reliance on solid techniques and combinations of ingredients which work together harmoniously is really the basis for any lasting cuisine.

On the other hand, it is Northern California's newer, more innovative chefs who have brought the area its new fame and glory as a culinary center. While methods and techniques of cooking have not changed measurably in recent years, what has changed is the way in which ingredients are utilized and mingled. Most of the area's newer chefs are bringing fresh attitudes, free from dogma, to their kitchens, and many are applying age-old techniques in the creation of exciting, new dishes.

One of the primary attractions luring so much talent to Northern California is the availability of some of the world's finest quality, freshest produce. Northern California seems to have it all. We are blessed with a salt water ocean and bay as well as fresh water lakes and rivers nearby, all of which provide an extraordinary range of fresh seafood. The Central Valley of California offers an abundance of the freshest vegetables and fruits as well. Because of strong local interest, there are sources for more exotic edibles ranging from quail, boar, squab, poussin, pheasant, and venison to baby leeks, shiitake mushrooms, and all of the fresh herbs. We have, in California, a truly bountiful feast, and many farmers and growers are specializing in producing ingredients specifically for quality-conscious chefs.

Another factor in Northern California's emergence as a major culinary area is the proximity of numerous grape-growing and winemaking regions. Centuries of tradition have married good food with fine wine, and it was inevitable that in Northern California both would experience big growth spurts simultaneously.

Whether anything can be identified as "California cuisine" at this point in time remains a question. It will probably take many more years before we can assess whether a lasting cuisine has really developed. However, there is clearly a renaissance in the culinary arts which has been developing over the past five to ten years in California. It has to do with utilizing the wealth of natural food products available, and it is reflected in a fresh, innovative approach to cooking which embodies traditional techniques without the burden of rigid tradition that often comes with them. It is the instinctual sense of knowing what to do with quality ingredients which characterizes the great chefs who are developing our evolving cuisine.

Years ago, good food was just good food. What has emerged in recent years, partially through the efforts of the French proponents of *nouvelle cuisine*, Henri Gault and Christian Millau, is that the chef has finally come out of the kitchen, both in his physical presence and in the chef's personally-styled plates. The chef has been thrust into the public limelight and has become a superstar of sorts—a new hero for the 80's. No longer is he or she some faceless character stuck in a sweaty kitchen. The eating public wants to know: Who created this dish? Just as it was impossible for Picasso or Van Gogh to remain anonymous, so it has developed with contemporary chefs. Such is the evolution of the culinary arts.

The chefs (and restaurants) chosen for inclusion in this book run the gamut from classically-trained to self-taught; from those making a strong personal statement with their food to those who cook to feed empty bellies; and from the slim and trim to those who obviously enjoy too much of their own cooking. The geographic range is from San Francisco northward with the major emphasis on the Bay Area itself.

The specific choices of chefs and restaurants are arbitrary and subjective based on my 37 years of dining experience in Northern California. I remember well as a kid the first smells of the oak-burning oven at Lupo's (now Tomasso's) and the smell of fresh fish at Fisherman's Wharf before it found its way to Tadich's or Sam's where we'd gobble it up. I also recollect my first samplings of fine French food and realized that there was something more to eating than filling your stomach. The choices seemed endless then, and are far more so now.

My goal in writing this book was to choose a cross-section of traditions, styles, and philosophies of cooking to offer a broad overview rather than focus simply on French chefs or even the "Best of" approach, which this book only partially attempts to do. Eating means different things to different people. We'll find that cooking does too. And so begins the search for "the spirit of cooking".

THE NUTRITIONAL, SPIRITUAL, & MEDICINAL VALUE OF WINE

By: Mike Grgich, Grgich Hills Winery

My experiences with wine as a nutritional beverage began very early in my life as a dietary supplement in place of milk. Wine was the major drink in my family, and our annual consumption was approximately 50 gallons per year per person. My love affair with wine has been going on ever since I was a child, and gets better all the time, which is more than can be said for most love affairs.

Mama would never use Chlorine to sterilize water, but wine instead. About half and half was called "bevanda". By adding half wine to water, the pH of the water would usually drop from 6 to below $4^1/2$, and this controlled the growth of pathogenics or bacteria, which do not grow in liquids with pH below $4^1/2$. So I grew up knowing the value of wine both as a food and as a medicine.

Wine is important in the life of man because of the intricate chemistry of the grape, which is both a biological and botanical phenomenon. It is the world's most ancient beverage, and it has been an important medicinal agent in the history of mankind.

The use of wine as food and medicine has been celebrated in literature. In the Bible, Paul advises Timothy, "Drink no more water, but use a little wine for thy stomach's sake." Pasteur has written, "Wine is the most healthful and hygienic of beverages." President Thomas Jefferson, an avid wine collector, wrote, "Good wine is a necessity of life." The wise and witty Benjamin Franklin said, "Wine is proof that God loves us, and loves to see us happy."

So wine has great nutritional, historical, social, biological, psychological, and medicinal value. A glass of wine sipped after the day's activities gives time to recover from the pressures of the day, so that the psyche may be better able to cope with our frantic mode of life. Wine also gives man the desire to live against odds which might otherwise seem insurmountable.

Wine contains two basic types of food elements: 1) those providing energy (alcohol, sugar), and 2) those contributing to the maintenance of the body and its nutrition. About 95% of the alcohol is available for energy. Dextrose and levulose in grapes and wine are very important for energy and nutrition, and levulose is essential for the maintenance of the liver.

The nutrients in wine—amino acids, vitamins and all 13 elements which Underwood considered necessary for human life—are used by the body for proper nutritional maintenance. The potassium, phosphate and copper regularly found in wine are of significance in maintaining the rhythmicity of the heartbeat.

Wine, when consumed with food, adds digestive assistance. When you eat meat, you need to drink wine to help neutralize the fats in your stomach. When you swallow meat or fish, you get more from it if you combine that taste with the flavor of the wine. It sharpens your appetite by cleansing your palate and taste buds, and you are ready to eat more.

There is also a wonderful feeling as the wine is being swallowed. All of your senses are brought alive by the wine; you get a feeling of well-being and enjoyment. Since you are happier, you eat with a better appetite. Wine is both a physical and spiritual enhancement of yourself which brings into focus the goodness of life.

Food is more nourishing where wine is enjoyed, for the two interact and compliment one another. The combination of wine with food is like a good marriage—each enhances the other so there is perfect harmony and balance. Wine is a God-given gift to enjoy.

At Grgich Hills, we try to make wines that never overpower the food. We try to keep the acid, oak, fruit, alcohol and body in perfect balance. You don't taste the components of wine and food separately; they must be married together in harmony. Then they will lift your spirits higher and give you serenity and joy. Sipping an elegant wine with a well-prepared meal is one of life's most perfect experiences.

The Chefs & Restaurants

ALEJANDRO'S SOCIEDAD GASTRONÓMICA
Chef & Owner: Alejandro Espinosa

With the multitude of Latin restaurants in San Francisco, it's surprising to find one which combines traditional forms of Spanish, Peruvian, and Mexican cooking under one roof and makes them all work. Alejandro's is that kind of place—international, cosmopolitan, and jumping all the time.

The driving force behind this vision is Alejandro (Alex) Espinosa, a Spanish Jew from Peru, who was first inspired to cook by an uncle who "performed magic in the kitchen". Alejandro has since created an exciting blend of traditional Latin dishes from various countries and serves them from a kitchen which exudes vitality and energy.

Alejandro explains his beginnings: "I always dreamed of having my own restaurant where I could offer people the amount, the quality, and the atmosphere without squeezing their money. I thought I'd put the three kitchens together and serve the best dishes from each cuisine. I was particularly surprised at how the Peruvian dishes caught on because people didn't know much about that type of food. It's influenced by Spanish cooking. We were dominated for 200 years so we are still influenced. We have the Creole cuisine of Peru which is an Inca style of old cooking with foods like dehydrated potatoes and corn. Peruvian food also includes a lot of seafood which is why we like to do things like our *Ceviche* and *Paella*."

What troubles the diner at Alejandro's is making the choice of what to eat since so many dishes are special. Appetizers like *Alejandrinos* (won-ton type pastries filled with melted cheese, eggs, and jalapeños), *Ceviche* (marinated white fish in lemon and onions which is lightly cooked with pink still showing), or dishes like *Trucha "Meson de Candido"* (a whole trout stuffed with Serrano ham), or any of the superbly prepared Mexican dishes all tempt the diner. But it is Alejandro's *Paella Valenciana* which is his signature dish.

Alejandro explains what makes his *Paella* so special: "We use all fresh seafood like crab and mussels. The chorizo sausage is made in California by Spanish Portuguese. We use expensive, imported Spanish saffron, which they hand pick the threads from the blossom of the flower. Then we grind all of our own spices in the kitchen. I also have eight cooks working with me. We have a system where we first cook it in the frying pan, and then we put it in the paella dish and let it dry over a very low fire. It works out very well."

Alejandro sums up the rewards he gets from the hard work: "I always get personal satisfaction every time I cook a dish that comes out well. It's my reputation and all the years of hard work—I don't want to lose that! I have good, young cooks who want to learn. I get letters. I get great reviews, but most of all I walk through the restaurant and people applaud me. To me, that means the most—it means I created something which makes me proud and which gives satisfaction to someone else. I haven't fulfilled my dream yet, but I'm making progress."

PAELLA VALENCIANA

1/2 cup olive oil

2 cloves garlic, pressed

1 medium onion, diced

1 medium tomato, chopped

1 medium bell pepper, cut julienne style

4 pieces chicken (4 oz. each)

8 1″ cubes salt pork

1 1/2 cups long-grain rice, rinsed

4 cups water

1 medium size Dungeness crab (cleaned, cracked, but uncooked, including butter from inside shell)

4 - 8 medium size prawns, including heads

4 steamer clams in shell, scrubbed

4 calamari, cleaned and cut in 1″ pieces

4 small links Spanish sausage (chorizo)

1/2 tsp. salt

1/4 tsp. white pepper

2 whole bay leaves

Dash Spanish saffron (threads or powder)

Heat oil in heavy skillet and brown garlic. Add onion, tomato, and bell pepper and continue to cook. Add chicken and salt pork and brown. Stir in rice, then add water and turn heat up. Bring to boil.

Add seafood, including crab "butter", sausage, and seasonings. Reduce heat and simmer 30 - 45 minutes.

Serve in an earthenware pot or paella dish.

Serves 4 - 6

THE BUREAU OF FISH AND GAME
Chef & Owner: Mark Stech-Novak

The word "artist" is an often misused term, particularly when applied to the world of cooking. There are many fine craftsmen, even some very good technicians, but few real "artists"—chefs with a unique vision and flair for originality. Mark Stech-Novak, who recently left his position as executive chef of both the intimate French restaurant, Le St. Tropez, and the bustling midtown San Francisco grill, Camargue, truly fits the bill.

While many chefs lay stake to originality with exotic ingredients and pretentious *nouvelle* preperation, Mark Stech-Novak does it with a vivid imagination and an eye for plate decoration. His plates are like walking through a museum of modern art—the styles range from bold Impressionism to almost sublime Japanese fine art. Each plate is individually prepared and decorated with the main dish itself plus an array of garnishes and swirled purées. The work is done with a fine hand and a loving eye, and the effect is breathtaking.

This is not to say that Stech-Novak's fascination with plate design is all fanfare and no substance since his uniquely personal style of cooking is only embellished by his gorgeous plates. A number of dishes in his previous restaurants hit on a distinctly European-Oriental feeling. For example, *Crepinettes* were prepared using chicken, prawns, clams, cilantro, red chili, ginger, and garlic and served on a bed of Italian *cappelini* with a sauce of eggs, butter, sesame oil and a reduction of sea kelp, bonita flakes, and rice wine vinegar.

Stech-Novak, who was trained as an enologist at the University of Dijon after cooking stints at Chez Michel and the Squire Room at the Fairmont Hotel, speaks of his search for character in his food, "I like to think that I create dishes and use cooking techniques that are sensible and without pretense. If I make salmon with crayfish sauce, I want the plate to shout "SALMON" and "CRAYFISH" and "FLAVOR"!! Whispers and subdued tastes are usually lost in the mouths of modern diners."

Stech-Novak recently travelled in France and experienced seven 3-Star restaurants, which seems to have altered his point-of-view: "I really had my eyes opened in France. Perhaps I will be a little more subtle with my cooking than before. Like with a beautiful painting, sometimes the vision can get a little too complicated."

While Mark Stech-Novak makes plans for his new restaurant, The Bureau of Fish and Game, he remains pragmatic: "The art of cooking and the business of making money in a restaurant are often murderous bedfellows. Making sense and then making good food out of all of it is quite a challenge. I feel there is a grand but simple logic to well-prepared food; it is harmonious, appealing, and satisfying. Therefore it enrichens one's life. I like being rich—even if only in this sense."

MALLARD DUCK WITH RHUBARB

1 Mallard duck

1 bay leaf

2 - 4 juniper berries

1/2 cup water

4 cups rhubarb, chopped in 1/2" dice

3/4 cup sugar

1 stick of cinnamon

2 cloves

Salt and white pepper

You will need a pot with a tight lid, such as a Dutch oven or highsided oval casserole, in which to cook the duck. Skin the entire duck, saving all the fat. Cut the skin in 2" squares and place with the fat and bay leaf, juniper berries, and water. Cook either in the oven alongside the pan with the rest of the duck or on the stove. Simmer until all the fat has rendered and is clear and limpid.

Chop rhubarb and mix with sugar, cinnamon and cloves. Salt and white pepper the inside and outside of the duck. Pack with rhubarb mixture. Put some of the mixture in the bottom of the dutch oven, place the duck on top, and cover with the remaining rhubarb. Bake for approximately 1 1/2 hours at 325° with a tight fitting cover.

Remove the duck and bone off the legs and thighs and carve the breasts from the cage. Keep warm while you reduce the rhubarb mixture to a puree consistency, removing the cinnamon and cloves. Turn the heat up under the skins and cook until crisp and savory. Remove from the fat and drain on paper towels and salt like potato chips.

Present the pieces of duck on the rhubarb puree, sprinkled with the skins.

Serves 4.

CAFE ROYALE

Chef: Farnham Hogue   Owner: Sam DuVall

It might be difficult getting past the beautiful Art Deco decor of one of San Francisco's most stylistic restaurants before you realize how good the food is at Cafe Royale. But despite the plush, 30's elegance of the restaurant, the cuisine is innovative, exciting, and totally modern.

Sam DuVall, owner of the Elite Cafe and Cafe Royale, has created a memorable environment for what he calls "modern cooking for today's taste". DuVall is candid about his motivation, "This is the kind of food I like to eat because it doesn't fit into the confines of definition. We're not interested in what's cute, or exotic, or trendy. We just use good, basic ingredients prepared in a way which titillates the tastebuds and brings out the natural flavors of the product."

Salmon comes from Norway, baby scallops from Georgia, fresh oysters and pompano from Florida, and mussels from Maine. DuVall says, "The *nouvelle* movement has had the tendency to throw together a lot of incongruous items in a rush to create something new and different, but what you get a lot of the time is a hodge-podge of ideas that don't really work."

In charge of the kitchen at Cafe Royale is Farnham Hogue, a young chef who worked at Scott's, the Sonoma Mission Inn, and Sutter 500 with Roger Verge, before being lured to Cafe Royale by DuVall. Hogue describes his inspiration for cooking: "Since I studied photography in school, I see cooking as a kind of "instant art"—You have a vision; you create it; you present it; people say "ahhh", and then it's gone. It's like a performance piece. But there's real artistry in all this for me and a certain amount of ego too."

"What I'm doing here is a more contemporary kind of food. It's the food of the 80's in terms of what people are looking for in their diet and in terms of style of the plate. The public today has evolved greatly in terms of what it wants to eat. People are looking for things like Conch Chowder rather than basic Clam Chowder, for example."

Dishes like *Smoked Roasted Lamb with Cabbage & Bacon, Smoked Chicken & Green Apple Salad, or Eastern Swordfish Steak with Black Pepper/Lemon Sauce* are not pretentious at Cafe Royale. They are both attractive and tasty—the kind of food which inspires and satisfies. You remember these dishes long after you've eaten them.

Hogue seems keenly aware of his role as a young, innovative chef: "What I have to do is maintain my reputation because I have myself on the line with every dish that comes out of the kitchen. I do my best work under pressure, and I create a certain amount of pressure just to keep myself producing the most consistent quality I possibly can. To do that I have to attack it with a certain amount of verve and passion, and that is what makes it exciting."

BRAISED PRAWNS IN CABBAGE LEAVES WITH CAVIAR IN A WHITE WINE BUTTER SAUCE

$^{1}/_{2}$ cup white wine
2 Tbs. shallots, chopped
1 Tbs. white wine vinegar
$^{1}/_{2}$ cup cream
$^{1}/_{2}$ lb. sweet butter, softened
Lemon juice to taste
16 U-15 prawns

8 Napa cabbage leaves
6 Tbs. chives, chopped
1 cup leeks, julienned
4 Tbs. flour
Salt and pepper to taste
4 tspn. caviar

Combine white wine, shallots, and vinegar in a saucepan and reduce over medium heat until liquid becomes a glaze. Add cream and reduce by half. Over a very low heat, whisk in softened butter, a tablespoon at a time. Remove from heat and add lemon juice. Hold at room temperature until needed.

Clean and devein prawns, remove tails. Blanch cabbage leaves. Chop chives and julienned leeks. Assemble packets by laying out cabbage flat and then place a teaspoon of chives and a small bunch of leeks on each leaf. Place two prawns on each leaf and season with salt and pepper. Wrap cabbage leaves around prawns.

As you are folding the last edge of the leaf, pat it with a little flour to hold it closed.

In a sauté pan, add a tablespoon of butter and a pinch of shallots. Add prawn packets to pan and cook in butter for 30 seconds. Add a little white wine and water to pan and simmer for 30 seconds. Cover pan for 3 minutes over low heat.

Remove cabbage packets and place on towel to drain. Pour butter sauce on a warm plate and place packets on middle of plate. Garnish each packet with a $^{1}/_{2}$ tspn. of caviar and sprinkle a little chives on both sides of the plate.

Serves 4.

CALIFORNIA CULINARY ACADEMY

Head Chef: Jean Luc Chassereau   Owner: McKesson Corporation

Where else can you sit in a spacious, airy dining room and watch 100 people through large plate glass windows prepare and serve your food? The California Culinary Academy is the brainchild of Danielle Carlisle, a former biology research assistant at Stanford, who started CCA in order to provide a place in San Francisco where aspiring chefs could receive European training without having to go to Europe. What evolved is a serious culinary school headed by some of Europe's most experienced chefs, which doubles as a first-class restaurant to channel the output of the teaching process.

During a sixteen month program for the price of $8,800, students can learn all phases of Continental cooking with the anticipation and hope that their investment will pay off in the real world. The California Culinary Academy is a large model of what to expect, and both the instruction and the cooking are intensive. Classes start at 7 AM and continue until late in the day. All phases of preparation and cooking are taught. Some students double as waiters and waitresses to help defray some of the cost of the school until such time as they graduate and look for work.

Head Chef Jean Luc Chassereau talks about what it takes to be a chef, "To be a chef you have to love cooking, people, and the basic ingredients. It's like a gift of affection. It's also half chemistry and half art, which means you have to follow a recipe and know how the ingredients will merge together. Then, you want to create a dish that looks attractive and tastes good. Cooking is like painting. You have a palette. You have your primary colors. And you have to understand how the colors work together so you can make your own colors. But first you have to understand basics before you can create."

The kitchen at CCA seethes with activity— day and night. The curiosity of the students and enthusiasm of the chefs creates a dynamic teaching and cooking environment. Looking in from the dining room, you feel almost voyeuristic, and there is an inevitable sense of theater.

The food at CCA, while hard to classify, can be strikingly original. Such dishes as *Sautéed Squab with Wilted Escarole, Bacon and Cherise Sauce* or *Broiled New York Steak with Oyster Sauce and Macadamia Nuts* appear on the ever-changing menu. Chef Chassereau, who worked at Maxim's in Paris and at René Verdon's Le Trianon in San Francisco before joining CCA says, "We have so many fresh food products available here in California to which we apply basic European techniques but with open minds and objectives. I love cooking because you can never get bored with it. There's always something new to learn, and that's what we try to teach our students here."

ENTRECOTE AUX HERBS (MARINADE)

1 New York Steak (6 to 7 oz.)

1-2 Tbs. butter, clarified

1/4 cup cognac

1/4 cup cream

1/8 cup demi-glace or brown stock

1 pinch chopped fines herbes (thyme, sage, basil, chives, and chervil)

Sauté the steak in clarified butter and cook to taste. Place steak on a dish and keep warm. Deglaze pan with cognac and add cream and demi-glace or stock. Add chopped herbs. Reduce and mix with butter and cover the steak. Season with salt and pepper.

Serves 1.

CAMPTON PLACE HOTEL

Chef: Bradley Ogden   Owner: William Wilkinson - Ayala Hotels

Bradley Ogden, the 31-year old chef at the elegant, new Campton Place Hotel on Union Square, may be the most important new chef to arrive in the Bay Area in quite some time. Ogden, who ventured West from the successful American Restaurant in Kansas City, is an amiable, enthusiastic man whose food sensibility is strongly affected by the simple fare he grew up with at home in Travers City, Michigan ("the cherry capital of the world").

"I still think about that pan-fried trout straight out of the lake but now I'm trying to do it with a little creativity," he explains. "My dad was a great cook. I remember eating his homemade fudge while playing Monopoly at home, and I recently asked him for his Orange Chiffon Cake recipe which we may integrate into the menu."

Ogden's perceptions of American cuisine reflect a clear understanding of how to use good, fresh ingredients in an appealing, creative manner. Now that Ogden is in the Bay Area, he has access to more of these ingredients than ever before. Delicacies like quail from Half Moon Bay and Sonoma bacon, which is smoked with no preservatives, show up in his dishes.

"American cooking is old recipes like your grandmother used to make, but it's also using recipes she didn't have. American cuisine is so influenced by other cultures anyway. We're trying to develop a simplicity here starting with French technique but using mostly high quality American ingredients. Cooking is mostly instinct and a feeling for what works together. You probably won't see me, for example, using kiwi with lobster, but I do like to experiment."

Campton Place offers a menu which primarily emphasizes the strengths of its chef. A *Crab Chowder* redefines the state-of-the-art in chowder creations with its thick crab chunks and flavorful base with hints of bacon and Idaho potatoes. *Spiny Lobster with Blue Corn Cakes* is a glorious combination of poached local lobster with blue corn cakes (from blue corn, indigenous to the Southwest). A *Grilled Quail* is marinated and grilled, and is then served with smoky bacon slices on a bed of fried, shoestring, sweet potatoes. The dish is startling in its simplicity, yet intriguing and complex in flavors.

Brad Ogden is humble and unpretentious—a clean-cut, American boy if there ever was one. While both the public and local chefs have greeted him enthusiastically, he remains steadfast and determined: "To be successful and consistently good, you have to be committed. We're doing three meals a day at the hotel, and those two eggs over easy are just as important as any other dish. I'm a little amazed at our success so far, but we still have a long way to go."

CRAB CHOWDER

Poaching:

1 whole crab (about 3 pounds)

1/2 cup brandy

1 cup sherry

2 quarts clam juice

8 parsley stems

4 bay leaves

1 Tbs. garlic, minced

4 Tbs. shallots, minced

Chowder:

1/2 cup salt pork, rind removed and diced 1/8"

1/2 cup bacon, cut into small strips

2 cups onions, chopped

1 1/2 cups celery, diced 1/4"

1 Tbs. thyme

1 1/2 cups all purpose flour

3 cups heavy cream

2 cups Idaho potatoes, peeled, diced 1/2" and blanched in lightly salted water

Seasonings:

1 Tbs. kosher salt

1 tspn. ground white pepper

1/2 tspn. tabasco sauce

Place all ingredients for poaching in a stock pot, cover and bring to a boil. Skim and cook gently for 12-15 minutes or until crab is cooked. Remove crab from liquid, crack and bone the crab, leaving meat in large flakes. Reserve for the finished soup. Strain the poaching liquid through a fine strainer or cheese cloth and reserve for soup.

In a heavy bottomed pot, combine salt pork and bacon. Place on high heat and cook until meat is crispy and the fat is rendered. Add celery and onions and sauté on medium heat for about 8 minutes or until the vegetables are tender. Add thyme and flour to the vegetable mixture to make a roux. Cook at low heat for 5 minutes. Slowly add the poaching liquid while stirring constantly until all the liquid has been absorbed. Simmer lightly for 20 minutes, add cream, potatoes, and seasonings.

To serve, add the crab meat and garnish with chopped parsley.

Serves 12-14.

LE CASTEL
Chef: Emile Waldteufel   Owner: Fritz Frankel

Of all the outstanding food available in San Francisco, surprisingly, the style of cuisine that comes up a little short is classic French. Not that there's not enough to choose from, but comparitively few restaurants deliver the traditional tastes with all the refinements.

Le Castel, a beautiful, high-styled Victorian, is the creation of consummate restaurateur, Fritz Frankel, who came to San Francisco via Brenners Park Hotel in Switzerland, the Ritz in Montreal, and the Claridge in London. Frankel finally opened Le Castel after successful stints at Trader Vic's and his own La Mirabelle.

Frankel obviously takes a lot of pride in the classic presentation at Le Castel, "I like light, fine cooking but not *nouvelle cuisine*, which I find a little gimmicky —serving half the portion for double the price. What we do is find the best and freshest ingredients, and they become the basis for everything we do."

Frankel and Chef Emile Waldteufel have created a menu which partially reflects the chef's Alsatian family background. Dishes such as *Stuffed Squab with Fresh Cabbage, Leg of Veal with Horseradish Sauce,* and *Fresh Seafood in Puff Pastry* truly shine in the hands of the hard-working Waldteufel. He comments, "It's always a challenge to see something work. You're continually striving to make it a little better than the last time. For example, I'm always trying to bring out the flavor of a sauce a little more so that it can enhance whatever it's being served with. It's experimental to a certain extent. I finish sauces for each individual dish. That keeps me on my toes and sharper because I keep tasting, tasting, and never taking it for granted."

Waldteufel, an accomplished bicyclist, who rode in the 120-mile marathon in the 1972 Summer Olympics in Munich, is the kind of organized worker who seems totally captivated and obsessed when he is cooking. His plate decorations, while not lavish are extremely attractive.

Chef Waldteufel is obviously committed to his role in the kitchen: "Personally, it thrills me when I see someone happy. At first I wasn't sure I'd like the military discipline in the kitchen, but when I developed some confidence, it became challenging to work fast and be accurate with a degree of finesse at the same time. Sometimes you might want to throw a pan across the kitchen when things get too busy, but that's just for the moment. Overall, I wind up feeling good, particularly when the dish comes out just right."

CHANTERELLE MUSHROOMS ON TOAST

1 1/4 lbs. chanterelle mushrooms, cleaned and sliced

1 Tbs. finely chopped shallots

1 Tbs. finely diced bacon, lightly browned

1 French baguette

Glaçage:

1 Tbs. butter

1 1/2 Tbs. flour

1 cup milk

1/8 tspn. salt and white pepper to taste

Bay leaf

Pinch of nutmeg

2 medium size egg yolks

3/4 lbs. drawn butter

Squeeze of fresh lemon

Salt and white pepper to taste

1 cup whipped cream

3/4 cup port wine

6 Tbs. unsalted butter

Fresh ground pepper

Clean chanterelles with a brush or rinse quickly in cold water and then slice. The mushrooms should be firm and dry. Cook shallots and bacon until lightly browned. Cut baguette in 12 pieces diagonally 1/4″ thick. Spread butter on one side and lightly toast both sides.

For glaçage, make a béchamel by melting 1 Tbs. butter in a saucepan over low heat. Blend in 1 1/2 Tbs. flour and cook slowly, stirring for 2 minutes. Do not allow mixture to color. When mixture has cooled, bring milk and 1/8 tspn. salt and white pepper, nutmeg, and a bay leaf to a boil and mix with butter and flour mixture (roux) with wire whisk. Cook over medium-high heat and whisk until boiling. Boil for 1 minute while stirring. Remove from heat. Strain.

Prepare hollandaise made from 2 medium size egg yolks, oil from 3/4 lbs. drawn butter, a squeeze of fresh lemon, salt and white pepper to taste.

Whip one cup of cream. Strain hot béchamel into a mixing bowl. Add the hollandaise and mix. Add the whipped cream and mix gently. (Note: the glaçage should be used while it is warm otherwise it may separate when glazed.)

Heat 6 Tbs. unsalted butter in a sauté pan with enough surface to accommodate the chanterelles confortably. Add the chanterelles, shallots, and bacon. Sauté over a high heat until mushrooms have a glazed appearance. Add port wine and reduce to half. Add 1 1/2 cups of demi-glace, salt, and fresh pepper to taste.

To serve: cover the face of four plates with a layer of glaçage and place under a broiler until the glaze becomes light brown. Arrange three slices of toast on each plate and spoon a mound of hot chanterelles on each piece.

Garnish with watercress and serve immediately.

Serves 4.

CHEZ PANISSE

Part-Time Chef & Owner: Alice Waters   Head Chef: Paul Bertolli

A hundred years from now, when the development of cooking in the 20th century is being chronicled, it's likely that the name Alice Waters will be discussed almost as much as it is today. Alice Waters, creator and guiding spirit of Chez Panisse in Berkeley, is arguably the most influential culinary figure in Northern California.

Waters pioneered a new era of cooking in the 1970's which emphasized fresh, local ingredients, utilized and combined in imaginative ways. This may have been the beginnings of what is now being exploited and imitated as "California cuisine". But, the truth is that Alice Waters' heart, soul, and palate are entrenched in the cobblestone villages of the Provencal area of Southern France where she was first inspired as a cook.

When she was 19, Waters travelled to France "having never really eaten anything". There, she wound up meeting new people and "eating all the time". She still reflects on the beautiful simplicity of an experience in an old stone house in Brittany: "The trout had just come from the stream and the raspberries from the garden. It was fresh and direct from the source, and the conviviality of home cooking that I felt there was something we try very hard to capture in our restaurant now."

Another inspiration was Elizabeth David's *French Country Cooking,* and Waters promptly cooked every dish in it. Upon her return to the U.S., she cooked at home for awhile, but finally gave in to her obsession and opened Chez Panisse (named after a character in Marcel Pagnol's French film classic) in 1971. All she really wanted was a place to cook for her friends, but, unexpectedly things took off for Alice Waters and Chez Panisse.

Waters has alternated as chef and owner of the restaurant over its turbulent 12-year history. Currently, Paul Bertolli, a tall, handsome, ex-pianist with an Italian cooking heritage runs the kitchen. Waters observes, "When Paul first applied for a job, he was rather flamboyant with nasturtiums. But then he went to Italy and started doing things like making his own olive oil and vinegar. He came back very inspired, and I hired him in 1982. He's got the gutsy taste I like—olive oil, vinegar, anchovies, and garlic. He makes everything taste good!"

Part of what makes Chez Panisse so fascinating is its bold, adventuresome, free-wheeling spirit. Where else can you find dishes like *Artichoke Soup with Hazelnuts, Grilled Boned Quail with Beet Puree & Potato Croquettes,* and *Chocolate Torte with Blood Orange Creme Anglaise* all on the same evening's menu?

Waters is passionate in her philosophy of cooking: "Food is getting back to basics. To feel the reality of cooking with totally hand-processed, fresh, nutritional food is very inspiring and cathartic. Smelling, tasting, and using all the senses is so important. So much is lost in the mechanization of cooking. You've got to feel how the garlic is hot on the tips of your fingers to really understand food."

SPIT-ROASTED SQUAB WITH ANCHOVY-OLIVE BUTTER

3 fresh squabs

2 onions

1/2 bunch parsley

2 cups red wine

1/3 cup brandy

Olive oil

3 whole salt-packed anchovies

1 cup pitted Niçoise olives

1/4 pound butter

Salt and pepper to taste

Marinate 3 fresh squabs with 2 sliced onions, 1/2 bunch parsley, 2 cups red wine, 1/4 cup brandy, and a little olive oil for several hours, turning frequently.

To make the olive-anchovy butter, fillet 3 salt-packed anchovies and rinse them thoroughly under cold water. Pound them in a mortar with 1 cup pitted Niçoise olives, 1/4 pound butter and the remaining brandy.

Spit the birds so that they are securely fastened on the skewer. Place the birds over a hot grill or next to a hot fire. As they turn, they should be basted with the marinade. Depending on the size of the birds and the heat of the fire, they should take about 20-30 minutes and should have a crisp brown exterior and rare interior.

Allow the squabs to rest after cooking. Cut them in half and spread the pieces with the olive-anchovy butter.

Serves 6.

CHINA MOON

Chef: Barbara Tropp   *Owners: Barbara Tropp & Paul Bernstein*

For someone who grew up on T.V. dinners, wheat germ milk shakes, and with Chinese dolls, Barbara Tropp has come a long way. Raised in New Jersey and trained as a Chinese scholar in poetry and art history, Barbara Tropp's first flirtation with food came during a two-year stay in Taiwan. There she lived with an old Chinese gourmand, Po-Fu, who introduced her to the art of eating. "In China, food is celebration. It was complete emotional liberation for me," she explains. Tropp's experiences eating from street vendors and shopping in Taiwanese markets helped form the foundation for what has become a complete love and obsession with Chinese food.

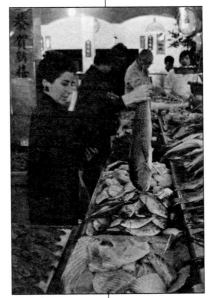

As her interest in cooking snow-balled, Tropp eventually moved to San Francisco and began teaching and writing a book on Chinese cooking while developing her local Chinatown food sources. Tropp explains, "The book borrows directly from the wonderfully eclectic Chinese kitchens in which I was such an enthusiastic and hungry observer. Thus it mixes the tastes of Hunan, Shanghai, Peking and Yangchow, and reflects the refined sensibility of an older generation of Chinese. The food is not fatty or sweet, or burdened with canned ingredients and fussy garnishes. It is lively, fresh and simple—zesty food that bespeaks my own temperament as well as that of my mentors."

Tropp is opening her own restaurant, China Moon, in mid-1984, and promises to open eyes and arouse palates. Her own style of Chinese cooking integrates many Western and specifically California ingredients, such as Anaheim chili peppers, Meyer lemons, and French baguette bread, with traditional Chinese techniques like stir-frying, smoking, pan-frying, and steaming. She reflects, "My own style is rather straightforward and singular. Authenticity means little to me. I care about taste. If a *Beggar's Chicken* is stuffed with canned bamboo shoots, canned water chestnuts, and canned ginko nuts and is served with a gloppy brown sauce, then it runs amuck of the whole tradition and philosophy of Chinese cooking. Freshness and a lively interplay of flavors and textures are what is important to a Chinese cook. In California, that means stuffing the same chicken with local wild mushrooms, red bell peppers and black walnuts. Then the gods will smile."

Other exciting dishes are planned such as *Pan-Fried Scallion Bread* ("the chewy kind of flat bread redolent of scallions that is eaten on street corners in Hunan"), sand pot casseroles of chicken and fresh water chestnuts, spare rib stews with garlic, and *Stir-Fried Rice Noodles with Curried Pork and Red Scallions*. China Moon will be a bistro with French influences, too, like sorbets made of Meyer lemons and Tropp's *Yin-Yang Raspberry and Mandarin Orange Tart*—all of which will be prepared in an open kitchen.

The Chinese concept of "yin-yang" or dynamic balance pops up a lot in Barbara Tropp's plans for her new restaurant. "I want to bring the spirit and flavor of real Chinese food into my restaurant," she emphasizes. "Chinese food, like the painting and poetry I studied, is predicated upon the idea that opposites come together in a harmonious but dynamic way. It's the juxtaposition of mild and spicy dishes that gives the cuisine its flavor and depth. You should taste—your tongue should sing—and your belly should be full."

SOURDOUGH CHICKEN TOASTS

1 lb. cubed boneless fresh chicken breast
1^1/2 Tbs. rendered chicken fat *
2 Tbs. cold water
1 Tbs. finely minced fresh ginger
1 hefty whole scallion, finely minced
1^1/2 tspn. old-fashioned coarse kosher salt
^{1}/8 tspn. Szechwan peppercorn powder **
1 Tbs. Chinese rice wine or dry sherry
8 fresh water chestnuts, cut to a small peppercorn-size dice (or ^{1}/2 cup tiny-dice jicama)

1 large egg white, beaten until stiff
20-25 diagonal slices of sourdough baguette, cut about ^{1}/2 " thin and 2^1/2 " long, and dried in 250° oven until both cut sides are dry
Small coriander leaves, black sesame seeds, and finely minced hot or sweet red fresh peppers, to garnish
4 cups corn or peanut oil for deep-frying

In a food processor fitted with the steel knife, mix the chicken, fat, water, ginger, scallion, salt, peppercorn powder, and wine until completely smooth. Transfer to a bowl, stir in the water chestnuts to combine, then fold in the egg white.

Using a small sandwich spatula, mound the puree on top of each toast to create a smooth plateau that is evenly ^{1}/2 " thick and rounded at the edges where it meets the toast.

To garnish, press a coriander leaf gently in the center of the puree and lightly sprinkle sesame seeds at one end and chili at the other.

To fry, heat the oil in a wok or broad, heavy skillet until a bit of puree floats to the surface within 3-4 seconds, 350° on a deep-fry thermometer. Slip the toasts into the oil one by one, puree side down, frying as many as

can float freely on the surface at once and adjusting the heat so they bob quickly to the surface. Fry until golden, about 2 minutes, then turn over to lightly brown the bread, about 15 seconds. Drain bread side down on a baking sheet lined with a triple thickness of paper towels.

Serve on a heated platter of contrasting color, garnished with fresh coriander and perhaps a cluster of fresh chilies.

*To render chicken fat easily and cleanly, simply cube the fat and steam it in a covered container over moderate heat until liquid.
**To make Szechwan peppercorn powder, heat the hollow peppercorns in a dry skillet over moderately low heat, stirring until fragrant, about 3-4 minutes. Pulverize in a mortar, then sieve to remove husks.

Serves 6-10, as appetizer.

COQUELICOT

Chef: Maxime Schacher   Owners: Maxime & Susan Schacher

In virtually every great dining city in the world, there is at least one tiny, out-of-the-way spot which serves incomparably delicious food but remains relatively unknown. These are the kinds of places which are usually shared secrets amongst knowing gourmets. Little Coquelicot, tucked away in pastoral Ross in Marin County, is just such a place.

Swiss-born chef Maxime Schacher and his wife, Susan, are the inspirations behind this cozy, unpretentious restaurant, and the food coming out of the kitchen reflects the best classic techniques combined with Schacher's bold, imaginative personal style.

Schacher was trained in Lausanne, Switzerland and worked throughout Europe in a variety of different capacities before landing in the United States at Restaurant Au Relais in Sonoma. From there, it was to the Hotel St. Francis, Restaurant La Mirabelle, and Chez Michel with a brief stop at the Hotel Princess Heiata in Tahita. Finally, Schacher opened his own restaurant in 1982 and is firmly planted in the Bay Area restaurant scene.

Schacher's style reflects a variety of influences. It is certainly based on classic French traditions: the sauces are rich and flavorful, and the techniques of preparation are familiar. Each sauce is prepared from a stock from the bone of the fish, fowl, or meat. However, many personal touches creep in—sometimes a Polynesian influence, other times a daring *nouvelle* twist with unique ingredients and lovely plate decorations.

To taste Schacher's food is to know his love for its creation. His execution always emphasizes natural flavors. A *Smoked Oregon Trout in Honey Sauce with Pickled Cantaloupe* is as skillfully prepared as a *Confit of Rabbit with Olives and Green and Red Pepper*. Seafood dishes also show the chef's deft hand, well-trained palate, and flawless technique.

Whatever the influence, the finished product is always satisfying. Schacher comments, "I love to cook. I have a lot of fun playing with food, and I think I am good at it. Our food is fresh and good. It is spontaneous, and it is international."

OYSTERS SOUVENIR DE TAHAA

3 eggs

1 Tbs. each chopped fresh thyme, marjoram, mint, and oregano

1 Tbs. chopped shallots

1 Tbs. chopped parsley

1 cup bread crumbs

20 medium size oysters

2 Tbs. flour

1 Tbs. olive oil

1 Tbs. butter

Sauce:

4 Tbs. chopped shallots

8 oz. dry white wine

2 oz. lemon juice

4 oz. heavy cream

4 oz. butter

Salt and pepper to taste

Garnish:

4 half oyster shells

4 sprigs of parsley

2 limes, cut in half

1 Tbs. chopped chives

Beat eggs in a bowl and set aside. Add fresh herbs, including chopped shallots and parsley, to bread crumbs and set aside.

Shuck oysters and save juice. Remove oysters from shells and place them on a dry towel. Sprinkle both sides of the oysters with flour. Dip oysters in egg mixture and then into bread crumb/herb mixture. Place oysters on dry towel and place in refrigerator.

In sauce pan, cook 4 Tbs. shallots, white wine, oyster juice and lemon juice until all liquid has evaporated. Add cream and bring to a strong boil and then whip in butter with a whisk. Remove from heat, season to taste with salt and pepper, and strain through a fine sieve into another pan. Keep warm.

In large frying pan add 1 Tbs. olive oil and 1 Tbs. butter. Heat until butter sizzles. Add oysters and cook for 1 minute on each side. Oysters should be light brown in color and crispy on the outside. Remove oysters from pan. Place between paper towels.

Warm serving plates. For each serving pour "cream of shallots" sauce on plate. Place oyster half shell in the center with the garnish of parsley sprig and 1/2 lime. Arrange oysters in a circular pattern around the garnish. Serve immediately.

Serves 4.

ELITE CAFE
Chef: Thomas Brown
Owners: Sam DuVall, Rahaim Talai, & Tom Clendening

The Elite Cafe, San Francisco's premier Creole/Cajun restaurant is the brainchild of Bay area restaurateur, Sam DuVall, whose vision has helped turn the Elite into a roaring success. DuVall, a native of Mississippi, is a restaurant man from the word "go" (the Elite is his 11th in the Bay Area), and it clearly exemplifies his philosophy that "the food has to be great and must pique the curiosity of the customer if it's going to be successful."

DuVall also talks about something which he calls "taste memory"—a certain quality which makes people remember a dish long after they've left the restaurant. The Elite's *Blackened Redfish* is one of those dishes. It's a Cajun specialty, which combines mixed spices with fresh rock cod. The fish is then cooked in a scorching hot skillet very quickly to retain moisture in the fish while blackening the outside. The result is a complexity of flavors and texture which is uniquely memorable.

Behind the kitchen doors where the cooking takes place, Louisiana-born Thomas Brown presides over his gumbos and Creole sauces. Brown, who is primarily self-taught as a chef, learned most of his basic skills from his grandmother and aunt. His cooking philosophy displays a healthy dose of pragmatism: "Taste is the real thing. You can follow a recipe, but you have to taste it to know if it's right. Most chefs won't tell you everything. You have to sneak up on 'em and catch them doing it!"

Brown's *Bread Pudding with Bourbon Sauce* is a classic example of another traditional New Orleans dish, and uses day-old bread as its base. But Brown says, "It's the bourbon sauce which really kicks it off!" He points out, "Creole-style is nothing fancy. In New Orleans they start with cayenne and salt, and they stick to basics. Jambalaya is really a scrap dish of things collected from Monday through Friday. Nothing gets thrown away. There weren't any refrigerators back in the old days, so they cooked with everything."

The Elite Cafe, with its fresh oyster and shrimp bar in front, its lively atmosphere, and authentic down-home cooking, has brought a little bit of Bourbon Street to mid-town San Francisco. And the natives are eating it up!

NEW ORLEANS BREAD PUDDING WITH BOURBON SAUCE

1 loaf day-old French bread (1 1/2 lbs.)

1 cup sugar

1 cup raisins

1/2 cup pecans

2 Tbs. vanilla

1 1/2 quarts half-and-half

5 eggs

Cinnamon to taste

1/4 lb. butter

1/2 cup sugar

1/2 cup water

3 whole eggs

Bourbon to taste

Mix together in a large bowl, the bread, sugar, raisins, pecans, and vanilla, breaking up the bread in small pieces. Add half-and-half and eggs. Mix with your hands until very creamy and completely without lumps. Put in ceramic or metal baking dish. Sprinkle with cinnamon on top. Bake at 350° for 45 minutes or until lightly brown and crusty on top.

While bread pudding is baking, melt butter, sugar, and water in heavy saucepan and bring to a boil. Take off heat. When cooled, add 3 beaten eggs and bourbon to taste. Serve over bread pudding.

Serves 8.

ERNIE'S

Chef: Jacky Robert   *Owners: Victor & Roland Gotti*

While Ernie's has retained its reputation for many years of elegant dining in the classic French tradition, young Jacky Robert, the current chef at the famous restaurant, is an example of a classically-trained chef who is innovating with some inspired *nouvelle cuisine* dishes.

Robert learned cooking in a small village in Normandy, France from a family friend who was convinced that Robert was going to be a chef some day because of the boy's fascination with simple kitchen chores like peeling potatoes. Robert followed this predestination with stints at Prunier's and Maxim's in Paris, after which he cooked in Boston and Florida. But it wasn't until he got the Chef de Cuisine job at Ernie's in 1978 that he finally started defining and realizing his own personal style.

Robert talks about his evolution as a chef, "I realized that cooking was something other than traditional and classical. I think there's a middle ground between heavy sauces and those that taste like bouillon. I'm still basically conservative, but I like to remodel classical dishes like *Beef Wellington*, which I do with two different sauces—a *coulis* of truffles and a *beurre blanc*. However, something like *Poulet à la Crème de Poires et Endives* (Chicken with Pears and Endive) is more my own kind of *nouvelle* creation."

The grand, 19th century-styled, red chintz dining room at Ernie's speaks of years of fine dining which have preceded Robert. The elegance of the room provides the proper setting for Robert's stylistic creations. Robert observes, "The good thing about *nouvelle cuisine* is that you are served a plate which has been presented by the chef rather than by the waiter, as it was done for so long. This has helped bring out more of the personality and artistry of the chef."

Watching Robert work in the kitchen, you sense the years of discipline and training, but you also see the imagination running free. He hovers over a stock pot, smelling and tasting for complexity. He examines some fresh squabs which have just come in. He dips his finger in a sauce and ponders the taste. Robert, for a young man, has the confidence and look of a seasoned pro, yet it is the continual challenge of maintaining the tradition of this historic restaurant which inspires him.

POULET À LA CRÊME DE POIRES ET ENDIVES

2 cups chicken broth

2 ripe pears

4 chicken thighs or 2 chicken breast halves, skinned

Salt and freshly ground white pepper to taste

1 cup whipping cream

1 head Belgian endive, coarsely diced

Bring chicken broth to simmer in medium sauce pan. Peel and core pears; reserve peel. Cut pears in uniform pieces and add to broth. Poach uncovered until tender. Drain, reserving broth. Transfer pears to processor or blender and purée until smooth.

Combine broth and pear peelings in saucepan and bring to simmer. Season chicken with salt and pepper. Add to broth, cover and poach until just done. Keep chicken warm in broth.

Boil cream in saucepan until reduced to $1/2$ cup. Add pear purée and heat through. Strain through a sieve. Consistency should be like medium white sauce; if it seems too thick, stir in small amount of poaching liquid to thin.

Make bed of endive on each plate. Top with chicken and cover with sauce.

Serves 2.

FOURTH STREET GRILL
Chef & Owner: Mark Miller   Co-Owner: Susan Nelson

Who is Mark Miller anyway? An anthropologist with a background in Chinese art history, a "graduate" of the Chez Panisse kitchen, and a fantastically talented chef in his own right, Mark Miller might be described as a "man for all seasons". But, most of all, Miller is a dynamic person whose style of cooking is as individualistic as he is.

Miller, who worked under Alice Waters at legendary Chez Panisse for four years, started the Fourth Street Grill in 1978. The ever-changing, eclectic cuisine of the restaurant is merely a reflection of Miller's varied cultural background and interests. He explains, "I'm interested mostly in Third World, non-Western cuisine where strong, complex, direct flavors are so important. I'm particularly interested in Yucatan cuisine, which is derived from the Mayans. Any place where there was a great civilization, there usually was a great cuisine."

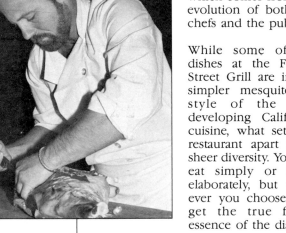

The integration of cooking heritages of many different countries and cultures is a trademark of Miller's unique, personal style. Accordingly, many of his dishes are seasoned or sauced with ingredients like turmeric, coriander, cardamom, preserved lemons, cloves, bay leaves, and chilies (he uses 16 different kinds in the restaurant). He borrows from the Mayans one week; the next week he may be working on a variation of a traditional Moroccan lamb sausage.

"I'm interested in expanding my repertoire and experimenting with a more flexible, improvised form. It's like the difference between classical and jazz music or like taking a folk melody and orchestrating it so that it still has its original vitality. You can't just invent it all yourself. I want to capture the spirit and preserve the integrity of the original cuisine and its flavors and develop an expanded palate."

Miller observes, "A culture is like a living organism. It learns, and when it learns enough, it develops into something of its own. We have the development of a food culture here in California in the last 10 years which comes from the evolution of both the chefs and the public."

While some of the dishes at the Fourth Street Grill are in the simpler mesquite-grill style of the still-developing California cuisine, what sets the restaurant apart is its sheer diversity. You can eat simply or more elaborately, but whatever you choose, you get the true flavor essence of the dish.

Seeing Miller operate in his kitchen, you sense the intensity of the man. He is not a chef who is easily satisfied. "I want to educate, not follow. To do that you have to expose people to more tastes. I don't want to be typified. I want to be free to move, and I want a certain intensity in my food. I want eating to be exciting. I don't want it to be comforting—it's not my personality," he admits.

LAMB SAUSAGE-MOROCCAN STYLE

2 1/2 lbs. lamb, with fat

1 1/2 lbs. pork butt

1/2 lb. back fat

2-3 bunches fresh coriander, with stems removed

1 Tbs. freshly ground cumin

1/2 cup currants, soaked in 1/3 cup white wine

3 large garlic cloves, minced

1 1/2 tspn. medium ground fresh black pepper

1 Tbs. salt

2 Tbs. Hungarian paprika

1 Tbs. cayenne

1 1/2 tspn. sugar

Medium grind meats. Hand chop coriander and toast cumin. Combine all ingredients and mix thoroughly. Put in medium size sausage casings or grill as patties over mesquite. Serve on a bed of lentils cooked with coriander and jalapeños.

Serves 8.

GEORGE'S SPECIALTIES
Chef & Owner: Angelina Semenoff

George's Specialties (named after Angelina's husband) is a hideaway of a Russian treasure on the edge of the Western world, and it offers the essence of homemade, old-fashioned Russian cooking. The lady who makes it happen, Angelina Semenoff, works out of a cubby-hole kitchen and painstakingly prepares virtually every dish from scratch. When you tell her that you love her *Chicken Kiev* or extraordinary *Beef Stroganoff*, her face lights up and she looks like she wants to hug you. To know Angelina Semenoff and to eat her food is to love her.

She describes her background, "From when I was a little girl I was always cooking. I loved to help my mama, and she taught me how to make beautiful things. We use to live in North China. Papa would cook Poltava borscht in the Southern Russian style—with meat, ham, bacon, and white beans. When mama died I became the main cook in the house. Then I eventually married a Siberian Cossack man who loved to cook too. We were always inventing and cooking all sorts of different dishes. We always had a dream to do something of our own. So, after we came to San Francisco, we opened this place first as a bakery and delicatessen, and people found out about us very fast."

In the kitchen, Mrs. Semenoff works slowly but lovingly. This kitchen scene is about as far removed from the rush and flurry of most larger kitchens as it possibly can be, yet the results speak for themselves.

Her menu is a virtual Hall of Fame of classic Russian dishes. *Borscht,* filled with beets and other fresh vegetables, is probably the best this side of Pietrograd, and other specialties such as fiery *Lamb Shashlik or Quail with Lingonberries* are fit for a Czar. While maintaining that it's just "simple food", there is a certain gourmet flair to her cooking. The dishes are all rich in flavor, consummately prepared, and, satisfying in every respect.

Semenoff defines her style succinctly, "I cook old Russian style, like they used to eat in old Russia when our Emperor was still alive. I don't know other cooking. I'm not interested in anything modern. I really care, and I want people to know old Russian food."

BORSCHT

10 beets, peeled and grated

5 carrots, peeled and grated

3 stalks celery, chopped

2 large parsnips, grated

1 1/2 cups oil

8 quarts water

Salt, pepper, and sugar to taste

1 large white cabbage, shredded

2-3 fresh tomatoes, diced

1 large potato, peeled and cut in cubes (optional: only if borscht is eaten the day it is made)

1 1/2 large onions, peeled and diced

2 Tbs. flour

12 oz. tomato paste

Peel and prepare all vegetables for cooking. Heat 1/2 cup oil in large sauté pan. Simmer one-half of beets, carrots, celery, and parsnips in oil without overcooking. Repeat with second half of vegetables.

Prepare a large pot with 8 quarts of boiling water. Add salt, pepper, and sugar.

In another saucepan, simmer onions in 1/2 cup oil until golden and add flour along with 12 oz. tomato paste. Add some additional water along with salt and sugar to taste. Stir until consistency is like pudding. Simmer for 5-10 minutes.

Then combine all pans together in a large pot and simmer for 10 minutes.

Serves 12.

GERTIE'S CHESAPEKE BAY CAFE
Chef: John Shields   Owners: John Shields & John Kelly

If John Shields' grandmother, Gertie, could see him now, she'd be real proud. Gertie used to drag her grandson around to church lunches in Baltimore where she cooked for businessmen in order to raise money for the church. That's exactly where Shields got his first impressions about food and cooking. What he remembers is that he peeled 200 pounds of potatoes a day, but "Gertie had real respect for food".

Shields is a young, energetic chef who cooked for six years at Berkeley's A La Carte before opening his own restaurant. He explains how he fits in to the California culinary world: "The whole mentality in California involves enormous respect for food. Back in Maryland, there was only one way to do things. It was semi-religious and dogmatic, and I didn't like it at all. Here in California there is so much to stimulate you as a chef."

His new restaurant is dedicated to the local cuisine of the Chesapeke Bay area where blue crabs are native to the waters. These crabs are smaller, more compact, and sweeter than Dungeness crab, and they are utilized in an astonishing number of variations from *Maryland Crab Soup* (a hearty vegetable-beef base soup with smoked ham hocks, fresh crab meat, and whole crab pieces) to the almost-legendary *Crab Cakes*, which have people driving 200 miles to taste them at Gertie's.

Gertie's is, unquestionably, crab-heaven. Transplanted Easterners are finding their way to the restaurant and creating havoc.

An order comes in to the kitchen for *Crab Cakes*. "How far did they drive?" Shields asks the waiter semi-kiddingly since the restaurant cannot get the quantity of blue crabs that it needs at the moment.

Crab Cakes are a delicacy indeed. Using meat from the back fin or lump fin, Shields combines eggs with "old bay", a blend of spices which includes allspice, pepper, and various grades of salt, and he uses cracker crumbs to bind. "It's definitely not health food," Shields confides. "The key is not handling the crab too much and deep-frying to get the right texture. This results in a succulent, flavorful inside and a crispy outer coating."

Gertie's *Maryland Crab Feast*, a healthy serving of crabs steamed with spices, drives customers into a frenzy. The table is lined with butcher paper, and you are presented with a wooden hammer, which is used as a cracking (read: bashing) implement to help extract the tender, juicy crab meat. This results in a kind of ritualistic, primordial display of eating.

With a twinkle in his eye, Shields says, "I think you have to be a little crazy to be a chef. We have a certain cohesive life here—almost a family atmosphere in the kitchen but with a great sense of pride. We're a tight group, but we're almost like misfits, cut off from the rest of the world."

John Shields has carved out a special presentation of American cuisine in Berkeley. His grandma must be smiling in heaven.

SAUTÉED SOFT SHELL CRABS

5 Tbs. unsalted butter

4 cleaned soft shell crabs (towel dried)

4 Tbs. fish stock

Pinch garlic, minced

Pinch shallots, minced

Juice of 1/2 lemon

Salt and pepper to taste

Heat butter in heavy pan over high heat. Lightly salt and pepper cleaned crabs. Place them in a pan skin side down and sauté for 1 minute. Turn over and sauté for 1 minute more. Remove to heated plate.

Pour out butter in pan and deglaze pan with fish stock. Over high heat, add garlic, shallots, and lemon juice. Salt and pepper to taste. Pour juices over crabs.

Serves 2.

GOLDEN TURTLE

Chef: Kim-Quy N. Tran   Owners: Kham Dinh & Kim-Quy N. Tran

Golden Turtle may be the best little Vietnamese find this side of Saigon. Run by Kham Dinh and Kham-Quy Tran, whose family owns a first-class hotel and restaurant in Saigon, the Golden Turtle is a typical San Francisco neighborhood restaurant which preserves its ethnic origins with a commitment to authenticity.

At the heart of the restaurant is Kim-Quy, a diminutive woman, who presides over her woks and grills with seeming joy. Her name literally translates to "Golden Turtle", which, according to legend, was a golden amphibian which inhabited a lake near Hanoi and was a symbol of good luck. Kim-Quy describes her background: "I come from a traditional family of restaurateurs from Central Vietnam. I was exposed to this type of cooking by my parents. Since this part of the United States offers choice ingredients, we are trying to bring another angle to Vietnamese cooking."

Catering to a clientele who have acquired a taste for Vietnamese cooking and want to further explore regional characteristics of this cuisine, Kim-Quy represents Central Vietnamese cooking and offers a choice of freshly prepared seafood and beef dishes in aromatic, flavorful sauces. Many of the dishes are barbecued, braised, or stir-fried. Contrasting colors, textures, flavors, and smells mingle harmoniously.

The couple shop for fresh ingredients every day, like it is done in Vietnam. Kham points out that even the coastline of Central Vietnam is comparable to the Bay Area and offers a similar variety of fresh seafood. Kim-Quy's outstanding *Sour Shrimp Soup* is a clear broth made from pork bones and contains fresh shrimp, tomatoes, onions, vinegar, fish sauce (a strong flavor used in Vietnamese cooking), lemon grass, coriander, garlic, basil, cumin, and pineapple chunks. The sweet, tart taste and aromatic spices send your senses swirling.

Another specialty, *Grilled Beef with Lemon Grass*, features a marinade with the unusual Oriental herb, lemon grass, which is a long, bulbous stalk that renders a pungent lemony-earthy aroma. It adds a delicate complexity to the thinly-sliced barbecued meat. Kham says, "I tried growing lemon grass here, but it doesn't seem to like the fog and coolness in San Francisco."

As you sit at Golden Turtle with its thatched roof, soft light, and pastoral murals, it's easy to imagine yourself right in Vietnam. When you sample the exotic preparations from Kim-Quy's kitchen, you feel another step closer.

PAN-FRIED DUNGENESS CRAB

1 whole Dungeness crab (1-2 lbs.)

1 egg yolk

1/4 tspn. salt

Sugar to taste

1/4 medium size onion

10 slices ginger

3 cloves garlic

3 Tbs. vegetable oil

2 tspn. Maggi seasoning (available in gourmet food stores)

Remove the shell from the crab and cut it into four equal pieces. Save the shell for decoration by heating in oven until it turns reddish. Be sure not to crack it. Place the yellow substance (crab butter or tomalley) from the shell in a small cup and mix with egg yolk. Season the pieces of crab with salt and sugar.

Chop onion, ginger, and garlic. In a large wok or pan, add the oil and wait until it starts to boil. Then stir-fry the chopped ingredients until the onion turns light brown. Add the pieces of crab meat and increase flame. Stir-fry for 3 minutes. Reduce to lower flame and add Maggi seasoning. Then add the mixture of egg yolk and yellow substance and stir-fry over high flame for 2 minutes.

Put pieces back to form original shape of crab. Pour stir-fried crab mixture over top and serve.

Serves 2.

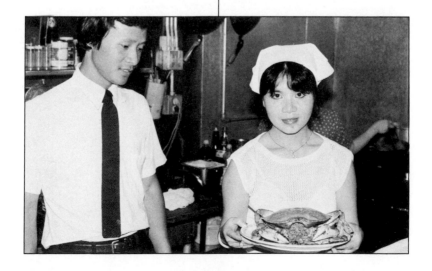

GREENS AT FORT MASON
Chef: Annie Somerville & Norm Fischer (Green Gulch Farm)
Owner: Zen Center

Mention vegetarian cooking to most gourmets, and you're likely to get raised eyebrows. After many of the dull, ill-fated ventures of the late 60's and early 70's, few food lovers get really excited about most vegetarian food. But Greens at Fort Mason raises the standard to almost transcendent heights, and in doing so it establishes a new form of cuisine based on seasonal freshness and innovation.

The real secret of Greens' success lies in the earth at the pastoral Green Gulch Farm in Marin County where Norm Fischer tends to the crops which produce the vegetables used at Greens. Fischer, a Zen Buddhist, explains the overall philosophy of Greens and the farm: "We developed our skills of vegetarian cooking as a by-product of our Zen practice. It's an attitude or a certain way we have of working together as a community that makes our cooking special. We believe in rotating jobs and doing different things as part of our practice. According to our master, Dogen Zenji, who taught in the 13th Century, working in a kitchen is a form of practice and training in traditional Buddhism. We believe that it's what you do, not just your contemplation, that counts."

The Green Gulch Farm provides a wide array of fresh vegetables, such as lettuces, chard, spinach, beets, cauliflower, and potatoes, which are integrated according to the season into the menu at Greens. The kitchen is currently run under the direction of Chef Annie Somerville, who offers a refined, diverse menu inspired occasionally by *provencal* cuisine.

Dishes like *Pizza with French Goat Cheese, Mozzarella and Romano Cheese, Red Onions, and Fresh Herbs* or *Brochettes of Marinated Tofu, Mushrooms, Tomatoes, and Peppers* (barbecued over mesquite charcoal) appear on the ever-changing menu. To say that the salads are fresh at Greens is a major understatement. All the greens at Greens resound with the natural flavor of the vegetable itself and are unlike anything found commercially. Greens also has a full-scale bakery within the restaurant which sells breads and assorted pastry delights from their Tassajara Bakery.

Take this breathtaking location over the San Francisco Bay, add a garden-fresh, natural approach, and solid culinary talent, and you have a winning combination. Greens is an evolving enterprise of some dynamic, spiritual individuals who are dedicated to their beliefs and to presenting top quality food.

MUSHROOM TIMBALE

1 cup diced yellow onions or 2 cups sliced leeks

1 Tbs. butter

2 cloves garlic, minced or pounded

1 1/2 pounds mushrooms, wash and pat dry

1/2 tspn. salt

1 1/3 cups milk

7 eggs

1/3 lb. gruyere cheese, grated

3/4 cup dried bread crumbs

Salt, pepper, and nutmeg to taste

Sauce:

2 Tbs. butter

2 Tbs. flour

2 cups milk

Salt and pepper to taste

2 Tbs. finely chopped parsley, chives, and thyme mixture

In a skillet, sauté onions or leeks in butter. Add garlic. Run mushrooms through food processor and add to sauté. Add approximately 1/2 tspn. salt. Cook mixture until liquid evaporates. Scald milk and set aside and let cool. Beat eggs and add to cooled milk along with gruyere cheese and mushroom-onion mixture.

Butter a loaf pan or ring mold and line inside with bread crumbs. Add remaining bread crumbs to timbale itself. Season with salt, pepper, and nutmeg to taste.

Bake at 350° in a bath of hot water for 50 minutes to one hour or until center is set.

To make sauce, make a roux with butter and flour. Heat milk and combine with roux. Season with salt and pepper to taste. Thin with milk if necessary. Add chopped herbs before serving over top of timbale.

Serves 6-8.

GULF COAST OYSTER BAR & SPECIALTY CO.
Chef & Owners: Dan & Carolyn Wormhoudt

Eating good, fresh seafood in the San Francisco Bay Area is not that difficult, but when you find a restaurant that imports the fresh seafood it serves, you know you've found something pretty special. The Gulf Coast Oyster Bar is just that kind of place.

Gulf Coast is the dream of Dan & Carolyn Wormhoudt, a husband/wife team from Louisiana who serve some of the most authentic Creole food west of New Orleans. Located in a rundown area of downtown Oakland, Gulf Coast is a clean, smart place which has the look of a typical California bar and grill. But the inspiration for the food digs deep into traditional Southern Louisiana cooking.

Dishes like *Crawfish Étouffée, Crawfish Bisque, Jambalaya, Dirty Rice*, several *Gumbos*, and *Redfish Courtbouillon* (pronounced "coo-bee-yon") evolved from Carolyn's family. The marinated and smoked chicken served at the restaurant originated from talks with Carolyn's grandfather about food preservation techniques which were common during his childhood in Morgan City, Louisiana.

Dan Wormhoudt discusses the preparation of *Redfish Courtbouillon*, "We use the Louisiana redfish, not local red snapper or red rock. I think that the special qualities of New Orleans cooking come from the characteristics of the seafood available in Louisiana as well as the procedures, preparation, and seasonings that generations of cooks have elaborated on for years. The practice of importing so much of our seafood is tremendously taxing, but I really feel that it's important to our cooking. That and the fact that we resist short cuts in our kitchen, like using Liquid Smoke or Kitchen Bouquet, is what makes our food special."

Creole dishes at the Gulf Coast exemplify the painstaking preparation utilizing all fresh stocks. The richness and spiciness of the *Jambalaya* or the *Gumbo* leave your taste buds tingling with fond memories long after the meal is over. A myriad of fresh clams and oysters are imported from the East Coast and Gulf Coast, and they are cracked fresh at the oyster bar in the front of the restaurant.

The Wormhoudt's and their staff have captured the essence of Louisiana Gulf cooking with uncompromising vitality, and their restaurant is a hallmark of these regional specialties.

SHRIMP CREOLE

15 lbs. fresh, ripe tomatoes (preferably Romas or Saladettes)

5 lbs. fresh head-on shrimp

4 cups medium yellow onions, peeled & finely chopped

3/4 cup good quality olive oil

1/2 cup inexpensive cream sherry

1 lb. butter (at room temperature or slightly cooler)

2 cups flour

1 1/2 cups medium bell peppers, stemmed, seeded, and finely chopped

1 1/2 cups celery, finely sliced (including some leaf, finely chopped)

1/4 cup fresh parsley, stemmed and very finely chopped

2 cups green onions, thinly sliced

1/2 cup garlic, minced

1 1/2 tspn. orange zest, finely grated

1/2 tspn. salt

1 tspn. cayenne

1/4 tspn. cloves, freshly ground

1/2 tspn. allspice, freshly ground

1 tspn. white pepper, freshly ground

1/2 tspn. nutmeg, freshly grated

1 cup dry red wine

1 tspn. blackstrap molasses

3 1/2 cups small "button" mushrooms, cleaned, stemmed, & quartered

2 cups baby carrots, peeled & julienned about 2 ″ in length

Pre-heat oven to 350°. Core, blanch, peel, seed, and coarsely chop 5 lbs. of the tomatoes and set aside. Head, peel, and de-vein shrimp, saving the heads and shells and covering and refrigerating the tails. Stem and coarsely chop the remaining 10 lbs. of tomatoes, conserving as much of the juice, pulp, and meat as possible. In a thick-walled pot on which a lid can be fitted, sauté 1/3 of the finely chopped onions and shrimp heads and shells in the olive oil. Use high heat, stirring briskly. When the shrimp parts turn pink, add the sherry, cook for 4-5 minutes, then add the chopped tomatoes. Cover the pot and place in the pre-heated oven for 1 1/2 hours.

While the stock is cooking in the oven, make a roux. In a thick-bottomed, thick-walled pot, combine the butter and flour over medium heat. Stir steadily and continuously with a whisk. Keep stirring until the roux is a thin liquid, about the consistency of olive oil. Keep whisking throughout the entire pot until roux turns the color of peanut butter, or a little darker.

Wearing a glove on your whisk hand, add the remaining onions. (There will be a burst of steam.) Immediately reduce heat to very low. Cook onions for 10 minutes, then add bell peppers, celery, parsley, green onions, and garlic, letting each cook for a few minutes before adding the next. Continue to stir the roux as vegetables are put into it.

When the stock is ready, strain it and add it a little at a time to the hot roux over a medium flame, whisking vigorously. When the stock is completely mixed, increase heat and bring mixture just to a boil, then reduce heat to a slow simmer. Add the chopped tomatoes, orange zest, and other seasonings, along with the red wine, and molasses. Simmer for 1 hour, adding the mushrooms and carrots for the last 15 minutes and the shrimp tails for the last 5 minutes.

Serve over white rice with a line of hollandaise if you have made it.

Serves 6-8.

HAYES STREET GRILL
Chefs: Anne Haskel & Patricia Unterman
Owners: Anne Haskel, Patricia Unterman, Robert Flaherty & Dick Sander

While the output of California's bountiful, fresh ingredients is seen in many local restaurants, nowhere is it more pronounced than at the Hayes Street Grill, which specializes in fresh seafood and salads but also offers a wide array of homemade pâtés, sausages, and desserts.

Chef/co-owner Anne Haskel, who was raised at home on "the Julia Child school of cooking" and travelled extensively in France, and partner, Patricia Unterman, a highly-respected food writer and critic, have combined their cooking skills and operate one of San Francisco's most popular seafood restaurants.

Haskel discusses the concept and origins of the restaurant in 1979: "We were looking for something with the old San Francisco feeling, like Tadich's but where the food is really special. Our food is simple, and it reflects Patty's and my taste based on all of our eating experiences. We have slightly different styles and palates—Patty is a little more influenced by Oriental flavors, based on her travels to Hong Kong and Bangkok, while I am more traditionally European-influenced, having grown up on quiches long before they were fashionable."

Fish can be ordinary, unless it's very fresh and prepared in interesting ways. While the menu at Hayes Street offers options, fish is the star. The restaurant uses an amazing variety, which is brought in daily by Paul Johnson of the Monterey Fish Company. Sturgeon, skate wings, mussels, salmon, scallops, Hawaiian tuna, New Zealand grouper, Florida red snapper, Delta crayfish, and Maryland softshell crabs all appear, depending on what's in season. Haskel says, "There's no limit to what we'll use as long as it's good. Our customers have evolved so much over the past five years that we can serve things now that we couldn't back then. Now they actually come looking for some of the more exotic foods."

Hayes Street Grill specializes in the use of mesquite charcoal which is imported from Mexico. The high heat that mesquite gives off allows the fish to cook fast and seals the juices, but the technique is more difficult than meets the eye. Haskel observes, "Mesquite is such a distinctive taste. It reminds me of eating grilled fish on the pier in Greece or Southern France. Cooking with it is tough since the fire has to be constantly stoked, with new wood being added to maintain the right temperature. The fish starts off at very high temperatures and then gets moved to the cooler side to finish. We find that some fish like lemon sole, petrale, and flounder taste better sautéed because the mesquite gives off too strong a taste."

With imaginative minds in the kitchen, the Hayes Street Grill captures the spirit of contemporary California cooking with sound techniques and direct, natural flavors.

MUSSELS WITH CREAM, CURRY & SPINACH

4 lbs. mussels

1 1/2 cups good fish stock

1 Tbs. curry

1 cup cream

2 bunches washed & trimmed spinach

Cook 1 lb. mussels in simmering fish stock for 1/2 hour. Strain and discard the mussels. Mix curry with cream and reduce by a third. Add to strained fish stock. Five minutes before serving, heat the liquid in a saucepan and add the remaining 3 lbs. of mussels and cover after 2 minutes. Stir and add the spinach. Stir again and cover for 2 minutes more. Ladle mussels into warm soup bowls and pour liquid on top.

Serves 6.

Ken Hom may be the smartest chef of all—he doesn't even have a restaurant. A fiercely independent and ambitious man, Ken Hom is a writer-teacher-photographer-art historian-food consultant-chef whose interests in cooking and culture lead him all over the world.

Hom has written a successful book, *Chinese Technique* (Simon & Schuster, $16.95/$12.95), which is an illustrated guide to the fundamentals of Chinese cooking based on Jacques Pepin's popular French book. He is currently working on a new book and an eight-part TV series for the BBC as well as another book called *The East-Meets-West Cookbook*. Hom also teaches and runs tours to Hong Kong. Not bad for someone raised on the poor side of Chicago.

His start in cooking was almost his end. Forced to clean 200 pounds of shrimp a day in his uncle's hot, sweaty Chinese kitchen in Chicago rather than "playing ball like the other kids", Hom rebelled and turned away from cooking until moving to Berkeley when he was twenty. Since then he has worked his way up the culinary ladder with a unique blending of traditional Chinese techniques with contemporary ideas and ingredients.

"Chinese cuisine is a known tradition which has been around for a long time," he explains. "What I am is a practitioner. The East-meets-West notion is how I apply myself as a Chinese-American. I am a creature of the West. I don't want to tamper with Chinese tradition, but much of the cooking is cumbersome and archaic—all the chopping and preparation. I want to be free to borrow from various sources."

Hom's interest in other cuisines has led him to develop such dishes him to develop such dishes as *Roast Loin of Pork with 5-spice powder, Thyme, and Orange Zest* or *White Corn-Scallion Soufflé with Ginger-Tomato Sauce.* Perhaps he will steam fish in basil or thyme, a very non-Chinese notion. Or, Hom might stir-fry duck livers and then de-glaze the wok with rice wine and shallots in the classic French method.

The man is enormously enthusiastic and seems to revel in and thrive on his own abundant energy. "My inspiration is cooking for friends because it's truly an act of love. That's one reason I've avoided working in a restaurant because I want to see who's eating my food and watch the expression on their faces as they eat," he explains.

"I like to cook with just the food in front of me. It's like making love—it's a sensuous process. It has to come from feeling, touching, and smelling. It has to come naturally, and when it doesn't, it usually doesn't come out right. Cooking is not an obsession with me—it's not an isolated discipline. It's inter-related with the rest of the world."

Whether Ken Hom, writer-teacher-world traveller, or Ken Hom, serious chef, winds up in his own restaurant is anybody's guess. What is certain is that wherever he is, he will be winning friends and influencing people with his bold, free-spirited brand of modern Chinese cooking.

STIR-FRIED SPINACH WITH GARLIC

3 lbs. fresh spinach

3 Tbs. good rich olive oil

2 tspn. salt

2 tspn. sugar

2 Tbs. garlic, very finely chopped

Wash the spinach thoroughly. Remove all stems, leaving just the leaves. Heat a large wok or pan to a moderate heat. Add the oil. Then add the salt and spinach. Stir-fry for about 2 minutes to coat the spinach leaves thoroughly with the oil and salt. When the spinach has wilted to about one third its size, add sugar and garlic and continue to stir-fry for another 4 minutes. Remove the spinach and pour off any excess liquid. Serve hot or cold.

Serves 4.

HUNAN RESTAURANT
Chef: Henry Chung

Bring on the fire engines! Henry Chung's Hunan Restaurant may serve some of the spiciest food in the world, containing varying amounts of red pepper oil, crushed red pepper, fermented black beans, minced garlic, and ginger. But that's only part of the story.

Henry and Diana Chung, a husband-wife team from the Hunan province in the South Central part of China (birth place of Chairman Mao Tse-tung), have created a working replica of food from their province in downtown San Francisco, and legions of fiery food fanatics fill the Hunan each day, just like the warriors who reputedly come from the Hunan province. Make no mistake — Hunan food is hot and spicy, but variations on the theme come in the form of smoked specialties such as ham, chicken, and duck, which are smoked the way Henry's grandmother did, using hickory wood, tea leaves, orange peel, rice husks, and Chinese five spice to achieve a powerful, country-smoked flavor.

Another famous dish, *Harvest Pork*, reputedly originates from the harvest season when plantation workers work so hard they need some kind of spicy, nutritious food to revive their utterly exhausted bodies.

Henry explains his personal motivation behind the creation of his restaurant, "Because my grandmother was a good cook and I have inherited quite a few unusual recipes from her, I want to share them with others. I am ever of the opinion that to serve the public and to make people happy should be everyone's obligation in order to make our place a better one to live." Henry further explains Hunanese tradition, "The unique taste of Hunan peppery dishes has made Hunan a topic for conversation. In addition, Hunan people are widely known for using longer chopsticks, larger plates and spoons, spacious tables, and oversized invitations which all may signify their generosity and hospitality. Hunan dishes feature both quality and quantity. Since most dishes are on the spicy and hot side, MSG is seldom or never used. Hunanese cooks and housewives consider using MSG a great shame to them."

The Hunan kitchen, guided by Henry and his son, is a marvel of stir-fry efficiency. High heat, lively seasonings, and quick hands mingle to create intriguing and enlivening dishes. Once called by *New Yorker Magazine*, "the best Chinese restaurant in the world", the Hunan may not be that, but it is a fun spot where your palate will get more than its share of red-hot chili peppers (known as "sky-facing peppers") and your stomach its share of good, authentic Hunan food.

Henry says, "Our food is spicy and hot, and it spurs actions in the body. In other words, our food gives extra life to our customers. It is good for young man. If one is not young, our food would make one feel young." Tasting is believing at the Hunan.

HOT & SOUR SOUP

5 - 6 cups chicken broth

1/4 cup tree ear or wood ear mushrooms, shredded (soak in warm water until soft - discard the stems and shred the caps.)

1 2 " square bean curd, chopped

1/4 cup bamboo shoots, shredded

1/2 cup dried pickled vegetables (imported from China)

1/2-1 Tbs. red hot crushed pepper (to taste)

1/4 pound lean pork, finely shredded and mixed well with 1/2 Tbs. cornstarch

1 - 3 Tbs. soy sauce (to taste)

Salt to taste

1 - 2 Tbs. vinegar (to taste)

4 Tbs. liquid cornstarch (mix 2 Tbs. cornstarch with 2 Tbs. cold water before using)

1 whole egg, stirred

1 tspn. sesame oil

1 scallion, finely minced

Boil the chicken broth; add mushrooms, bean curds, bamboo shoots, pickled vegetables, red hot pepper and pork. Keep stirring and bring to a full boil. Then add soy sauce, salt and vinegar to taste. Stir to mix well. Bring to a boil again and spread the liquid cornstarch slowly over the surface while stirring gently until the soup thickens. Reduce heat to medium high; slowly add the eggs to the simmering soup. Keep stirring until egg is floating on the surface. Remove to a serving bowl.

Garnish with the sesame oil and minced scallion. Serve very hot.

Serves 4.

KHAN TOKE

Chef: Areewan Fasudhani   *Owners: Areewan & Rangsan Fasudhani*

Going to little Khan Toke is kind of like taking your senses to the circus. There are so many exotic seasonings and ingredients used, that it's hard to know where the excitement will come from next. Khan Toke is the inspiration and vision of Areewan and Rangsan Fasudhani, a husband and wife team from Thailand, and it stands out like an Oriental jewel, sparkling in San Francisco's restaurant-laden Richmond District.

Khan Toke is an authentic, dimly-lit neighborhood restaurant with low tables and cushions where you check not only your coat but your shoes at the door. The kitchen, which is shockingly small, is a classic example of function and efficiency over size. The dishes are carefully conceived to present a series of thrilling taste sensations.

Rangsan elaborates, "We use a lot of different seasonings like lemon grass, laos, coriander root, Thai sweet basil, and ginger. These are all part of traditional Thai cuisine. We started Khan Toke because other restaurants prepare modern style—you sit in chairs. But we want to let the American people know about the old style Thai cuisine, the type served in the Thai Royal Palace. We use recipes from Areewan's family which she learned as a little girl."

Areewan, the delightful woman who runs the kitchen, comes from a long line of cooks and has been cooking for as long as she can remember. She still consults with her mother occasionally on recipes, and she receives periodic shipments of various curries from Thailand to use in her dishes.

One of Areewan's favorite dishes is a Thai crêpe called *Khanom Beung*, which is stuffed with shrimp, pork, shredded coconut, ground peanuts, Chinese radishes, bean sprouts and is served with a cucumber sauce. It is a marvel of sweet and spicy flavors and different textures. *Look Chin Moo Yang* (pork balls with Oriental fine herbs, which are wrapped in rice paper with ginger, garlic, and a sweet-spicy homemade tamarind sauce) is another example of the type of traditional dish which Areewan creates so superbly. Spicy Thai curries and barbecue specialties fare equally well in the minute kitchen. The amazing variety and consistency of the food at Khan Toke is the particular achievement of this talented couple.

Eating at Khan Toke and sampling the exotic fare is a sensation not likely to be forgotten, even after the hot peppers have worn off. Khan Toke is truly "the real thing" when it comes to authentic Thai cuisine, and you're not likely to find a better example of this type of cooking outside of Thailand itself.

KHANOM BEUNG (THAI CREPE)

Batter:

6 oz. rice flour

6 oz. all purpose flour

4 oz. coconut milk (Chaokoh Thai brand recommended)

$1/2$ tspn. turmeric

$1/2$ tspn. salt

4 oz. cold water

$1/2$ tspn. sugar

Stuffing:

2-3 tspn. oil

4 oz. ground pork

4 oz. fresh shrimp, chopped

8 oz. freshly ground coconut

2 oz. coriander root

$1/2$ tspn. black pepper

1 tspn. sugar

1 oz. citrus leaves (if available)

Orange food coloring

Cucumber sauce:

1 medium English cucumber, thinly sliced

1 medium red onion, thinly chopped

$1 1/2$ cups white vinegar

$1/4$ cup sugar

Thin slices of hot chili pepper (optional)

Garnish:

Bean sprouts, chopped Chinese radishes, chopped bean cake, and ground peanuts (to taste)

18 tspn. oil

To make batter, mix all ingredients in a blender until batter turns yellow and is smooth. Set aside to use for making crepe.

Prepare all ingredients by chopping and cutting as noted. To make stuffing, heat a couple of teaspoons of oil in an omelette pan, wok, or skillet. When hot, add pork and shrimp. Stir-fry for 5 minutes. Add the rest of the ingredients for the stuffing and continue to stir-fry for 5 minutes or until cooked. Remove from heat and set aside and keep warm.

To make cucumber sauce, mix all ingredients in a bowl and set aside.

To make crepe, heat pan and add 3 tspn. oil. Pour in 2 Tbs. of the mixed batter and tilt pan so that the batter coats pan and is spread evenly and thinly. When crisp at the edges, spread one side of the crepe with bean sprouts, then stuffing, and then other garnishes. Fold the other side of the crepe over filling. Turn crepe carefully and brown other side lightly. Repeat six times.

Serve with cucumber sauce over the top.

Serves 6.

KINOKAWA

Chef: Nobuo Sato   Owners: Hiroyuki Arakawa & Miss Noriko

The 1980's have seen the proliferation of the sushi bar phenomenon as one of America's latest food crazes. No doubt that the unabashed simplicity of fresh, raw fish prepared in an artful manner by master sushi chefs was something that took Americans some time to appreciate, but now almost every major American city has at least one sushi bar. In San Francisco, where there is a large Japanese population and a Japantown, there is an abundance of sushi bars, but nowhere is the fish any fresher or prepared more beautifully than at Kinokawa on Grant Ave.

The Kinokawa sushi menu reads like a "Who's Who" in the world of fresh fish. There is *Ika* (large squid), *Saba* (pickled mackerel), *Maguro* (tuna), *Ebi* (cooked prawns), *Tako* (octopus), and *Sake* (cured, smoked salmon) as well as many others. Variations are available with items like *Tamago* (egg custard), and *Maki-zushi* (sushi rice wrapped in dried seaweed with small chunks of ingredients in the middle).

Sushi evolved from the ancient Japanese tradition of layering fish and rice in a jar to preserve the fish. The fermentation of the fish rendered a tart, yet sweet taste to the rice. Contemporary sushi flavors reflect this ancient tradition.

While preparation looks deceptively simple, it takes very fresh fish and a fine carving hand to make it excel. Sushi chef Nobuo Sato works with the speed and efficiency of the world's best, yet he seems to rejoice in the delicate, loving caresses that he applies during the preparation. It takes just the right touch to create sushi, which is actually the mixture of vinegared rice, not the fish itself as is commonly believed. Salt, sugar, sweet rice wine, and vinegar must be carefully blended into the rice while it is fanned to cool. Timing is critical: The sushi rice mixture must be kept at body temperature after it is prepared in order to preserve its glossy, fresh look. Typically, the sushi is dipped in a mixture of *wasabi* (green horseradish paste) and soy sauce and is then eaten.

With sushi, it is the essence of the raw fish which really comes through, and it sometimes takes a developed palate to appreciate the subtlety. Chef Sato explains: "Everybody has a different tongue and taste. We have been trying to reach everyone to satisfy them. But it is really difficult. So our policy is: 'As long as the customer has a good tongue, he can pick a good taste'."

GYU-DON

2 cups soy sauce

1 cup sweet sake

1 cup water

3 tspn. sugar

12-16 oz. beef, shredded

1 onion, peeled & shredded

2 green onions, shredded

1 egg, sunnyside up

Handful of Japanese noodles (Ito-Konyaku brand recommended)

Pan fry all ingredients together 15-20 minutes. Serve over steamed rice.

Serves 4.

KOREAN PALACE
Chef & Owner: Nam Kun Song

Paul Bocuse, the famous French chef, equates the role of the chef in the kitchen to the conductor in a symphony orchestra, who must know what all the various sections are playing and must conduct them in harmony. Rather than a grand symphony conductor, Chef Nam Kun Song at the Korean Palace is a quiet artist, working sometimes in solitary on a beautiful vegetable or fruit masterpiece to garnish one of his dishes.

Nam Kun Song, and his wife, Un Hui, come from Taegu in South Korea, and the artistry and skill with which they run their lovely, understated restaurant is most impressive. After first opening an American restaurant in 1976, Song realized that he had to do something more personally satisfying. He comments, "There was not much known about Korean food here in San Francisco, but we decided to try it. At first we didn't have much success, but I decided to try introducing some attractive floral decorations with food as garnishes, which I had learned in a hotel in Seoul, Korea, and after that we started to catch on."

Song's cooking at the Korean Palace is unique and special, but it is the gorgeous *daikons* (white radishes) sculpted into floral shapes and Red Delicious apples transformed by hand into jagged towers which capture the eye and tell you that a master artist is at work. The actual creation of these masterpieces involves careful carving and slicing techniques which he applies with extraordinary speed and proficiency.

The dishes themselves range from the more well-known Korean specialty, *Kal Bi* (marinated beef short ribs) to various deep fried, pan fried, casserole, and steamed dishes. Song's style emphasizes many highly-seasoned and marinated dishes laced with hot peppers, garlic, sesame seed oil, and sugar. The elegance of the floral plate decorations provides an interesting counterpoint to the fiery impact of a sauce like *Kochoo jang* (red chilies and fermented soy bean paste), which accompanies some of Song's sautéed dishes. The recipes themselves are a combination of traditional Korean specialties and Song's original interpretations which he continually works to perfect.

Song explains, "Many people think that our food is derived from Chinese and Japanese cuisines, but Korea actually has a longer history than Japan. It's more likely that Japanese cuisine was influenced by Korean than the other way around. Now that people have learned a little about Korean food, they love it!"

KAL BI (BEEF SHORT RIBS)

4 lbs. beef short ribs (with bone)

1/2 cup soy sauce

4 Tbs. minced green onion

2 Tbs. minced garlic

3 Tbs. sesame oil

3 Tbs. sugar

3 Tbs. sesame seed

1 tspn. black pepper

Cut short ribs into 3" lengths and trim most fat. Slash the short ribs down to the bone in several places being careful not to separate the meat from the bone.

Combine all remaining ingredients for seasoning mixture in a bowl large enough to accommodate the short ribs. Add the ribs and mix thoroughly.

Marinate for 4 hours or more. Charcoal broil ribs over medium heat.

Serves 4.

MODESTO LANZONE'S
Chefs: Dale Cole (Opera Plaza) & Gino Laghi (Ghirardelli)
Owner: Modesto Lanzone

Modesto Lanzone, the dynamic owner of two magnificent Italian restaurants in San Francisco, is a kind of Renaissance man. He is an avid art collector, who built an entire new restaurant around his fabulous collection. He is a regular swimmer in chilly San Francisco Bay. And most of all, he is a food man of the highest caliber whose family background is intricately woven into the modern environment of his restaurants.

Lanzone was born in Genoa where "good food was always around our table". He grew up on typical Ligurian foods like minestrone, fresh fish, and seafood salads. In 1950 he came to the U.S. looking for new tastes and concepts in food. In the 70's he became a partner in famous Vanessi's in North Beach and then took over management of the struggling Julius' Castle on Telegraph Hill.

But Lanzone's independent spirit called, and he finally established his first restaurant in Ghirardelli Square to do "traditional Italian cuisine in a modern way". In 1982 he answered the call again and established his beautiful Opera Plaza location, which doubles as a gallery for his favorite modern art.

The food at Modesto Lanzone's runs the gamut from seafood salads to tastefully-prepared veal dishes using Wisconsin

veal. Other ingredients like Porcini mushrooms and white truffles from Italy are imported to help develop the refined menu. A dish like *Panzotti de Recco* (Stuffed Pasta with Ground Walnut and Ricotta) originates from Lanzone's home near Genoa where an abundance of walnut trees dictated that the walnuts had to be used sonehow, so they were ground and stuffed in pasta.

Lanzone picks and trains his chefs very carefully. "We work together to try to create perfection, but that's impossible, so we pick the best young chefs we can and train them well," he says. Dale Cole, his chef at Opera Plaza, impressed Lanzone because "he cooks very organized" while Chef Gino Laghi at Ghirardelli Square "is Italian and understands what we're trying to accomplish."

It's clear that food, wine, art, and people merge in some kind of magical way for Modesto Lanzone. He elaborates, "In order to be in this business and work 15 hours a day, you have to love what you do and create a good situation for yourself. It's more than just the ritual of serving food. For me, it's mostly interacting with people that's so stimulating. It gives me peace of mind so I can hit my bed at night and feel like I've accomplished something."

LOIN OF PORK WITH MILK

3 lbs. loin of pork without bone

$^2/_3$ cup carrot, finely minced

$^2/_3$ cup celery, finely minced

$^2/_3$ cup onion, finely minced

3 Tbs. parsley, finely minced

2 cloves garlic

1 sprig fresh rosemary

2 bay leaves

4 Tbs. olive oil

5 cups milk

4 Tbs. butter

2 Tbs. flour

Salt and pepper to taste

In a large heavy pan (just large enough for the meat), place the meat, all the vegetables, parsley, garlic, rosemary, bay leaves, and olive oil. Stirring constantly, sauté over moderately high heat for about 15 minutes.

Reduce heat and add the milk. Simmer over low heat, partially covered, for 2 hours. (This may be done in advance.)

Remove the meat. Pass the vegetable/milk mixture through a food mill (very fine) into a bowl. Clean large pan and melt the butter in it. Mix the flour to form a smooth paste. Gradually add the vegetable/milk mixture to make a sauce. Stir throughly.

Cut the meat into $1/4''$ slices and arrange a serving platter. Cover with sauce and serve immediately.

Note: Same recipe can be made with loin of veal.

Serves 6.

LEON'S BAR-BQ
Chef & Owner: Leon McHenry

Every once in awhile, when the taste buds scream for mercy from too much rich food, or when you're tired of fanciness and pretension, it's time to head for Leon's Bar-BQ for a soulful dose of the best barbecue in town. Leon's is a San Francisco institution and justifies its reputation by serving large, tasty portions of chicken, ribs, sausages, beans, and cornbread in the true, no-frills, Southern tradition.

Leon McHenry is an amiable, rotund man who started the first Leon's on Sloat Boulevard near the zoo in 1973 after first becoming addicted to a barbecue joint downtown and deciding that he could do it better himself. Leon hails from Oklahoma where his father was in the barbecue business, and his current barbecue sauce has evolved from his family and from much experimentation over the years. He observes, "Everyone cooks to their own personal taste. There are so many barbecue varieties available. I'm trying to create my own personal approach, and it happens to be what I like to eat. People get used to a certain taste; then you want to give them what they like and keep them satisfied."

Leon makes his barbecue sauce in large 12 gallon containers which provide for some 400 servings. He estimates the cost of his flavorful, spicy sauce to be around 17¢ per 4 oz. ladle serving. The essence of the smoky barbecue flavor does not come from the sauce alone, however. Leon uses what is called the "3 1/2 down rib", because of its location on the small, young pigs which are trucked in from South Dakota and Nebraska. The ribs are marinated overnight and then cooked in a special smoke oven heated by wood and hickory chips.

As you watch him working his smoke oven, choosing chicken and ribs to serve, and then ladling out healthy portions of his zesty sauce, you know that he could be doing nothing else. It's as perfect an American image as you can possibly imagine. Then, the taste of the tender, succulent ribs dripping in sauce takes you right back to childhood and makes you feel whole and alive.

Candid and unpretentious in his philosophy of cooking, Leon feels, "If you enjoy cooking, the long hours don't seem to matter. Seeing people enjoy your food is what really counts. No matter how hot it gets in the kitchen or how tired I am, it still makes me feel good when I see people munching on a plate of ribs with big smiles on their faces. Then I know I've done my job."

BARBECUED RIBS & BBQ SAUCE

3 1/2 lbs. pork ribs (will reduce to
1 1/2-2 lbs. after cooking)

Marinade:
1 Tbs. barbecue spices (can be found
in gourmet food stores)

BBQ Sauce: (Makes 4 cups)
1 small chopped onion
4 Tbs. oil
1 tspn. liquid smoke
4 Tbs. vinegar
4 Tbs. brown sugar
1/2 cup lemon juice
2 cups tomato paste

4 Tbs. Worcestershire sauce
1 tspn. prepared mustard
2 Tbs. beef base
1 cup water
1 tspn. paprika
2 Tbs. cayenne (optional for extra
hotness)
Corn starch (optional for extra
thickness)

Basting Liquid:
2 Tbs. vinegar
2 Tbs. Worcestershire sauce
2 Tbs. water

To prepare ribs, marinate in barbecue spices overnight. Do not refrigerate.

For sauce, brown onion in oil and add remaining ingredients. Cook until mixture boils. Then simmer for approximately 20 minutes. Add corn starch (mixed with water) for extra thickness if desired. The extra sauce can be kept in tightly sealed jars in a cooler or pantry.

To barbecue the ribs outdoors, cook over mesquite or charcoal for 15 minutes per-side, basting occasionally with vinegar, Worcestershire sauce, and water.

To cook in an oven, pre-heat the oven for 15 or 20 minutes, and then cook the ribs for 1 hour, basting occasionally at the end with the BBQ sauce.

Serve with BBQ sauce over top.

Serves 2.

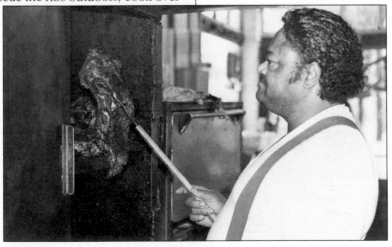

LIPIZZANER

Chef: Josef Roettig   Owners: Josef & Marianne Roettig

Tiny Lipizzaner is living proof that great, inspired food need not come out of a spacious, comfortable kitchen. Josef Roettig, a Viennese-trained chef with a classic French cooking background, works wonders out of a space which many chefs would consider the right size for a large walk-in refrigerator. What is more remarkable than the size of the Lipizzaner kitchen is the way in which Roettig organizes himself and his staff to work within the limits of the space.

Roettig trained in Vienna in all aspects of international cuisine and then took jobs cooking in top restaurants in various parts of Europe before coming to Ausin, Texas to open a French/Viennese restaurant. That undertaking didn't work out, so Roettig moved on to the Fairmont Hotel in San Francisco as Executive Chef and then to Hong Kong to consult with the Mandarin Hotel.

So it's not surprising that Roettig and his charming wife, Marianne, who manages the front, should finally decide to open their own restaurant. Roettig explains, "I wanted to have my own restaurant since I had always worked for other people in big hotel restaurants where I didn't have a chance to display my own personal style. We wanted to do something with a Viennese theme, but we didn't want anything in the German hofbrau-style.

Marianne and I worked on the menu very carefully to try to emphasize the things I do best in the kitchen."

What comes out of the Lipizzaner kitchen are classically-prepared French dishes with a streak of imagination and inspiration shining through. Clearly, Roettig is not interested in predictable kinds of dishes. A New Year's Eve dinner starts with a gorgeous, lavish *Lobster Parisienne*, moves into a *Consomme of Fresh Quail with Poached Quail Eggs*, is followed by a refreshing *Sherbet of Beaujolais Nouveau*, and is topped off with a beautifully-prepared, rich *Loin of Veal with Fresh Gooseliver*. This feast ends with a *Kentucky Limestone Lettuce Salad with Broiled Goat Cheese and Walnut Oil Dressing* and *Fresh Poached Pear in Pinot Noir with Raspberry Mousse and Sabayon of Champagne.*

The regular Lipizzaner menu offers classic Austrian *Wiener Schnitzel* and a warm Viennese crêpe as a bow to Roettig's origins, but the chef has opted for much more of an international scope (other than naming the restaurant after the famous Austrian stallions). Roettig's artistry and dedication impress with every dish that comes out of the kitchen. He comments, "Sure I cook to make a living, but we can use our years of experience to satisfy people, and I love to see them leave so happy."

SOUFFLÉ OF WILD RASPBERRIES & STRAWBERRIES

1 1/2 oz. raspberries

2 oz. wild strawberries

1/2 cup Kirschwasser

Butter

1 1/4 oz. granulated sugar

4 egg yolks

2 oz. powdered sugar

6 egg whites

Marinate the berries in kirsch for a few minutes.

Butter and sprinkle with granulated sugar six soufflé molds, size 3″ diameter and 1 1/2″ deep. Divide 2/3 of the berries into the six molds.

Whip egg yolks with powdered sugar until white. Whip egg whites until stiff adding the granulated sugar during the process. (Be sure to use a fat free bowl.)

Fold the egg whites carefully into the egg yolks together with the remaining 1/3 of the berries. As fast as possible, fill the mixture into a pastry bag and divide into the pre-set molds.

Preheat the oven to 375° and poach the soufflées in water for 30 minutes. Do not boil water. Unmold the soufflées on prewarmed plates and decorate as you wish with mint leaves or berry sauce.

Note: It is very important that from the moment the batter has been prepared the process be carried out to the end so that the soufflé does not fall.

Serves 6.

LITTLE JOE'S
Chef & Owner: Frank Montarello

Going to Little Joe's for a meal at any time of day is like taking a seat at the theater. You're full of anticipation, waiting for the curtain to open. In this case, it opens on Frank Montarello and his "faster than a speeding bullet" sauté chefs, who perform day in and day out for the throngs of hungry patrons who converge on this popular North Beach restaurant.

Little Joe's on Broadway is a less crowded version of the original, which Montarello opened in 1971 on Columbus Avenue, right off Broadway. Soon the crowds were too big and a move was made to expand the seating capacity. Still the lines formed outside. So, in 1982, Montarello opened the current Little Joe's, a larger space in an old pool hall with paintings of old San Francisco and photos of Montarello and his friends adorning the walls.

Personable and unassuming, Montarello describes his start in the business, "I used to dream about having a restaurant when I was in Italy. I was about fifteen then. We do old time Italian food here. We make *Veal Parmigiana* and *Scallopine*. They don't even make it like we do in Italy anymore."

Montarello cooks simple, unpretentious food with a flair, and he has one of the busiest lunch counters in the City. Watching him cook, the senses are dazzled. Oil is poured from what seems like the sky. Flames leap high in the air out of simmering sauté pans. The air starts to permeate with smells of garlic and fresh food. The action is in high gear, and as you sit at the counter and watch, you realize you are part of a dynamic interchange between the chef and the food. By the time it reaches you, your stomach's rumbling in anticipation.

The menu at Little Joe's is chock full of basic, soul-satisfying food like boiled meats, sautéed veal dishes, and pasta. Montarello obviously enjoys his visible spot in front of the stove at center stage: "I like serving fresh food with a lot of attention given to the ingredients used to prepare it. Most of all I like to see people happy eating my food. We cook in front of our patrons to preserve fresh taste, and that is very special. They get excited watching us prepare it, and we give them a delightful experience to remember."

CHICKEN LIVERS

Tomato Sauce:

1 onion, chopped

3 or 4 cloves garlic, chopped

1/2 rib celery, chopped

1/4 cup olive oil

Salt and pepper to taste

1 can (3 lbs.) Italian tomatoes, roughly chopped

1/4 cup chopped parsley

1 cup beef stock or 1 bouillon cube dissolved in 1 cup water

3/4 tspn. garlic

1 1/2 tspn. olive oil

1 lb. chicken livers

1 cup mushrooms

3/4 cup sliced onions

2 tspn. vinegar

1/2 cup chicken broth

Salt and pepper to taste

To make tomato sauce, in a 4 or 5-quart saucepan, sauté the onion, garlic, and celery in olive oil, sprinkling them lightly with salt and pepper. Cook them until the onion and celery are soft. Add the tomatoes, parsley, and beef stock. Bring to boil, reduce the heat, and let it simmer for 1 hour. Put the sauce through a grinder or a course sieve to retain a slightly rough texture. If a food processor is used, do not overprocess. For this recipe, you will need about 8 Tbs. of sauce. The rest can be frozen. To make chicken livers, lightly brown the garlic in olive oil. Add the chicken livers, mushrooms, and onions and brown. Add vinegar and cook for 1-2 minutes more. Add tomato sauce (8 Tbs.) and chicken broth. Reduce over medium-high heat for 5-7 minutes. Add salt and pepper to taste.

Serves 2.

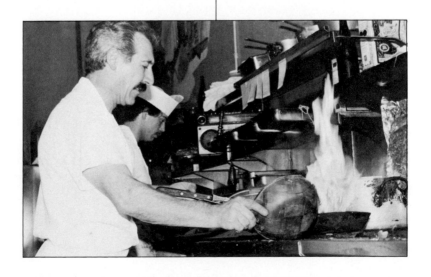

MAMOUNIA

Chef: Mehdi Ziani   Owners: Mehdi & Said Ziani

It's hard to imagine any other meal quite like what you encounter at Mamounia. First of all, there are no forks, knives, or spoons. In the true Moroccan tradition, everything is eaten with the hands. Then, you sit comfortably on the floor on soft pillows around a low table while you enjoy the exotic, highly-seasoned specialties of this little-known cuisine. Everything, from the low-lit, tent-like interior to the myriad of tastes which roll across your palate, is different at Mamounia.

Two Moroccan brothers from Rabat, Mehdi and Said Ziani , have re-created an authentic slice of Moroccan culture in a little hideaway-of-a-restaurant in San Francisco's Richmond district. Robust Mehdi Ziani, the chef at Mamounia, reveals why people like Moroccan food so much: "It reminds people of being little kids—sitting on pillows close together, eating with your hands, and getting close to the food. This is old home-style cooking. You have some sweet dishes, like *Lamb with Honey* or *Bastela* (pigeon pie, made with chicken in America) and some very spicy dishes like *Harira* (a Moroccan soup made with chick peas, lentils, lamb, and many spices). You are unlimited in the flavors you can experience here."

Moroccan cuisine involves a complex combination of spices such as cumin, cinnamon, coriander, turmeric, paprika and saffron with herbs like garlic, basil, onion, parsley, and mint. Each cook in Morocco has his own special trademark and method of preparation which has been passed down through the generations.

While claiming to have been "stuck in the kitchen for 30 years", Mehdi Ziani is obviously a man who loves food. He has perfected the technique of making his flaky filo crust for the *Bastela* by lightly coating the top of a hot, inverted skillet and gracefully peeling off the thin, cooked layer of filo before filling it.

The traditional Moroccan specialty, *Couscous* is laboriously created with 23 different ingredients to obtain its unique flavor. Likewise, Ziani's Moroccan bread, *L'Hobz*, is kneaded and rolled with the proficiency of a master baker. Lamb has a special place in Moroccan cuisine and culture, resulting from early Berber influences, and Ziani's love for it is evident in the many variations—lamb with honey, prunes, eggplant, onions, or brochette-style.

When the final drop of mint tea is poured into a glass from an ornate silver pot five feet above your head, the smell and taste send your senses into a world beyond. It is the fitting, soothing culmination to an exotic sensory experience—all at the hands of the dedicated Ziani brothers.

LAMB WITH PRUNES

1 lb. uncooked prunes

1 tspn. cinnamon

Water

2 Tbs. butter

1³/₄ oz. sesame seeds

4 lbs. lamb (any cut), trimmed of excess fat and cut into 2 ″pieces

1 tspn. salt

1 tspn. fresh ground black pepper

1 pinch saffron

³/₄ tspn. coriander

1 tspn. ginger

2 medium onions, peeled and finely chopped

1 cup oil

In a large saucepan, combine the prunes and cinnamon. Pour in cold water, adding enough to cover the prunes by 2 inches. Cook over moderate heat for ¹/₂ hour or until prunes are tender. Drain the cooked prunes into a colander, place them in a bowl and set aside.

In a small skillet, melt butter over medium heat. Add the sesame seeds and fry them until they turn a light golden brown (about six minutes). Drain the seeds on paper towels and set aside.

In a large casserole pan, combine the lamb, salt, pepper, saffron, coriander, ginger and minced onions; mix well. Add oil and brown all the ingredients, stirring frequently over medium heat. Add enough cold water to the browned ingredients to cover surface by one inch.

Cook over medium heat, stirring often, for 1¹/₂ hours, or until the lamb is tender. Stir the prunes into the other ingredients and simmer for 5 minutes longer. Place the lamb with the prunes on a large serving platter. Pour the sauce over the top; sprinkle with sesame seeds and serve.

Serves 10.

THE MANDARIN
Chef: Ki Kong Lau   Owner: Cecilia Chiang

Cecilia Chiang, the dynamic owner and guiding force of San Francisco's most elegant Chinese restaurant, The Mandarin, is a lady to be reckoned with. Madame Chiang was born in Shanghai as one of twelve children to a mother who "loved to cook and eat". However, Madame Chiang never entered the kitchen herself until her later years since tradition in China dictated that only servants did the cooking. After the Communists came to China in 1949, Madame Chiang moved to Tokyo where she started cooking Chinese food in her first restaurant, even though she didn't really know how to cook much at the time.

Since that time, Cecilia Chiang's rise to success in the United States has been stratospheric. She opened the first Mandarin on Polk Street in 1960 before moving to the current Mandarin location in Ghirardelli Square. There she first introduced a number of new Mandarin, Hunan, and Szechwan (correctly pronounced "Sutroyn") dishes to unknowing American palates. These dishes, *Sizzling Rice Soup, Prawns a la Szechwan,* and *Mu Shui Pork*, have since become standards in Chinese restaurants throughout the U.S., but nowhere are they cooked more expertly than at the Mandarin under Chef Ki Kong Lau.

The reason behind the enormous success of the restaurant is primarily Cecilia Chiang herself. A dedicated perfectionist, she explains her own philosophy: "Whenever I do anything I want to do

it right. Even now I still go into the kitchen constantly to taste the food and check the ingredients, and I've been in this business for 32 years. I also personally buy many of the fresh ingredients we use in Chinatown, so when the customer tells me how good the dish tastes, I know it's partly because I took the time to pick out fresh crab or lobster. Then I show the chefs how I want things done. We try a lot of new dishes, and we do traditional things too."

The Mandarin offers a number of specialties which reflect Madame Chiang's tastes. Her famous *Smoked Tea Duck* is marinated in star anise, Szechwan peppercorns, ginger, scallions, and water, then is trimmed of all fat and cooked in a wood smoke oven so that it absorbs the flavors of jasmine tea leaves and all the other smoked ducks which preceded it. The result is a moist but crispy duck, unlike anything most Americans have eaten.

While luxuriating in the beautiful Mandarin overlooking San Francisco Bay, one cannot help but marvel at the way in which the charming and charismatic Madame Chiang has built her restaurant. She reflects, "We've come a long way from when people thought Pot Stickers were Chinese raviolis. People's tastes have changed, and we're trying to present the best of Northern Chinese cooking in a relaxed setting. From this I get my own satisfaction. I love people . . . and you meet a lot of wonderful ones in this business."

BEEF A LA SZECHWAN

Marinade:

2 Tbs. soy sauce

1 Tbs. wine (or cooking sherry)

1 tspn. fresh minced ginger

1 tspn. sugar

1 lb. flank steak

2 stalks celery

1 large carrot, peeled

3 cups cottonseed oil (or any other light cooking oil)

Seasonings:

1 tspn. minced dried chili peppers

1 tspn. minced dried peppercorns

1 tspn. sesame oil

1 tspn. salt

Prepare marinade by mixing together soy sauce, wine, ginger, and sugar.

Trim the fat and membrane of the flank steak. Slice the meat across the grain into julienne strips. Place the meat into a bowl with the marinade for 1 hour.

Cut the celery and peeled carrot into julienne strips the same size as the beef.

Heat the oil in a wok until very hot. Place the marinated beef into the wok and stir fry the meat for about 10 minutes. Then reduce the heat and keep stirring until the meat becomes dark and dry (approximately 5 minutes). Take the beef out of the wok with a strainer and let the meat drain.

Remove most of the oil from the wok, leaving about 2 Tbs. Turn the heat high and stir fry the chili peppers. Add the carrots, cook for 1 minute, then add the celery and the beef. Stir fry for another minute, sprinkle on the peppercorns, sesame oil, salt and serve.

Serves 4-6.

MASA'S

Chef: Masataka Kobayashi   *Owners: Masataka Kobayashi & William Kimpton*

Few chefs in the world could expect the kind of instant acclaim Masataka Kobayashi experienced when first opening Masa's in the newly-renovated Vintage Court Hotel in July 1983. But Masa had blazed his culinary trails from Tokyo to Switzerland and then to France where he worked at the Hotel Meurice in Paris. He then migrated to the U.S. where he further established his reputation at Le Plaisir in New York. Finally, Masa moved to the Napa Valley and became chef at Claude Rouas' Auberge du Soleil before deciding to open his own smaller restaurant in downtown San Francisco. His legions of fans followed faithfully, and Masa's has quickly become one of San Francisco's premier dining spots.

Masa is a diminutive, 42--year old Japanese man who hardly looks like the celebrity chef he has reluctantly become. His dedication to classic French technique ("24 years . . . only one way") combined with Impressionistic plate garnishment have earned him this stature, but Masa is a quiet, humble man who works painstakingly to create his "edible art".

His interest in the visual look of his plates results partly from time he spent in Paris where he used to memorize details in paintings at the Louvre Museum. "I love bright colors and artists like Monet. I always keep a notebook and I write down ideas and sketches all the time. Sometimes in the middle of the night I'll get an idea and sketch the dish. Then, some time later, I may see some beautiful fresh fish or something which inspires me, and the whole concept will come together. Then we try it in the kitchen and if it works, we put it on the menu," Masa explains.

Since moving West, Masa has further developed his classic French dishes with many fresh California ingredients ("That's what attracted me here"), and the results are stunning. A magnificent *Pâtés Fraiches aux Truffles* (Linguini with Truffle Sauce) gives way to a *Poitrine de Faisan aux Morilles et Poire* (Breast of Pheasant with Morels and Pears). Likewise, Masa's desserts are captivating in their beauty and are sinfully delicious.

The look of these dishes may at first appear *nouvelle*, but the taste of Masa's sauces is far from it. He explains, "Nobody really knows about *nouvelle cuisine*. It will take years to develop. It started 50 years ago after Escoffier and developed later with Michel Guerard, Paul Bocuse, and the Troisgros brothers. I don't need crazy *nouvelle cuisine*. I believe basically in classic techniques but with new ideas."

At Masa's, the master is concentrating on serving 75 diners a night rather than the 200 he served at Auberge du Soleil. This allows him to concentrate on fine execution and elaborate plate presentations, aided by his excellent kitchen staff. "I spend energy cooking because I love it and it's my life. I have many ideas and recipes, but I'm not too fast. I'm the tortoise-type. I like to do things step-by-step. I don't use shortcuts. I want to do things the right way," he explains. "I had a dream one night in New York that I was cooking in California with fresh vegetables and all sorts of things. Now, here I am—my dream has come true. It's a beautiful story."

MUSTARD-GLAZED POUSSIN

1 poussin, about 1 pound

1/4 cup olive oil

1 Tbs. chopped shallot

1 Tbs. mixed fresh herbs, chopped

1/2 tspn. salt

Pinch of pepper

1 Tbs. mustard

1 tspn. olive oil

Juice of 1/4 lemon

Bone the poussin as follows: Cut along either side of the backbone and remove it. Cut through the underside of a thigh to expose the thigh bone. Scrape around the bone and remove it. Cut along a leg to expose the bone. Hack the leg bone about halfway down to break it. Remove only the portion closest to the thigh. Repeat with the other thigh.

Cut off the second and third joints of the wings. Place the chicken skinside down and hack at the wishbone to break it where it forms a "V". Bend the breasts back to pop out the keel bone. Peel away the remaining bones, leaving the first joint of the wing.

Finally, cut a notch in the bottom skin of one leg and slip the tip of the other leg through the slot so the bird holds its shape.

Marinate the poussin in 1/4 cup olive oil, shallots, herbs, salt and pepper for at least 10-15 minutes.

Grill the poussin skin side down over charcoal if possible. It may also be sautéed in oil and butter. After 5 minutes, turn the bird skin side up and paint it with a mixture of mustard, 1 tspn. olive oil, and lemon juice. Place the bird in a pan and under a broiler to brown the skin and cook it through, about 5 minutes.

Serve it on a plate garnished with fresh vegetables, steamed or boiled and well drained.

Serves 1.

MAURICE ET CHARLES' BISTROT

Chef: Marcel Cathala   *Owner: Maurice Amzallag*

While other French restaurants come and go in the Bay Area, Maurice et Charles' Bistrot has achieved near legendary status for its consistency and excellence. Charming Maurice Amzallag has established a casual yet elegant bistrot dining atmosphere and his partner, Chef Marcel Cathala, fills it with some truly unforgettable dishes.

Amzallag comments, "Once you have reached a certain level of excellence, the difficulty is to work to stay at that level and to work little by little to maintain consistency of cuisine, service, promptness, and courtesy—this idea that your customers should feel welcome." At Maurice et Charles', all the elements seem to blend harmoniously, but the real excitement is the food.

Young Marcel Cathala, who apprenticed at the 3-Star La Pere Bise in Tailloires, France, works out of a closet-size kitchen, and is typical of some of the younger French chefs in Northern California who use their classic training as a stepping-stone to creating a well-defined personal style. Dishes like *Caneton à la Graine de Cumin et au Miel* (skinless, boneless duckling with cumin and honey) and *Médaillons de Porcelet au Calvados* (young pork with apple jack brandy sauce) represent the restaurant's outstanding menu.

The sauces, in particular, shine. Richly flavorful, they are derived from expertly concocted stocks and are embellished with a knowing hand. Cathala explains, "When I brainstorm and develop something new, I like it, and I know it's good, usually the first time. I work to refine whatever I've done to make it perfect. Then, I put it in the book."

Cathala buzzes with enthusiasm about cooking: "I love to create. It's like an artist who paints a picture. You get satisfaction when you create something beautiful. Cooking is very individual and very complex. You're trying to achieve something personal, but you have to really work to discover it. But it's a great feeling to have customers come and tell you, 'Oh my dear, that was so wonderful!' They kiss me and tell me they love me. You need that kind of feedback to keep going."

FILET DE VEAU ST. ARMAND

Whole loin of veal, de-boned and trimmed

1 bunch spinach leaves, de-stemmed and blanched

4 slices bacon, raw

String

Garniture:

8 radishes, washed, trimmed with some top green attached

1 pint chicken stock (for vegetables)

2 summer squash, washed, dried, halved, then cut and fanned

2 cloves garlic

Fresh rosemary

Sauce:

1/2 cup white wine

2 shallots, chopped

1 cup demi-glace & deglazed pan juices

1 cup liquid from vegetable cooking liquid

1 Tbs. cornstarch, mixed with white wine

Salt and white pepper to taste

Lemon juice to taste

1-2 Tbs. coriander, chopped

1 tspn. butter

Salt and white pepper to taste

Butter

1/2 cup white wine

To prepare the veal, trim the loin completely, leaving it whole. Cover all over with blanched spinach leaves, preferably in one layer. Cover with bacon in a single layer. Tie up with string and set aside in refrigerator. (This can be done well in advance of cooking.)

To cook garniture, put radishes in 1 cup chicken stock. Bring to a boil, simmer 2 minutes and let sit in liquid for 1/2 hour. Remove 1/2 liquid for sauce. Then simmer summer squash in 1 cup chicken stock with garlic cloves and rosemary for 5-7 minutes. Remove 1/2 cup liquid for sauce.

To make the sauce, make a reduction of the white wine and shallots. Add demi-glaze. Add the vegetable cooking liquid

(chicken stock) and the deglazed pan juices. Bring to a boil, simmer 2 minutes and thicken with cornstarch. Bring to a boil again and simmer 2 minutes. Season with salt, white pepper, and a few drops of lemon juice. Strain and add chopped coriander and butter. Keep warm.

To cook the veal, season with salt and pepper. Sear on all sides in hot butter until colored. Place in 375° oven for 40-50 minutes. Remove veal from pan and set aside. Deglaze pan with white wine (1/2 cup) and add to sauce.

To serve, slice veal. Arrange in center of plate; cover with sauce. Place radish and summer squash at each end of plate.

Serves 4.

MIFUNE

Chef: Shigemitsu Shimane   Owner: Eiji Miwa

If you never thought that slurping your food could be considered proper, little Mifune in Japantown might pleasantly surprise you. Mifune is the home of the noodle—a Japanese fast-food, which is recreated proficiently at the restaurant by Chef Shigemitsu Shimane, who learned the art of making homemade noodles in Japan. Noodles have also been produced by the Miwa family of Osaka, who owns Mifune, for over 50 years.

There are two basic types of noodles which are served at Mifune— *udon*, thick, white noodles made from cake flour and *soba*, thin noodles made from buckwheat and hard flour. They are served in 31 different varieties—cold with dipping sauces or hot in soup combined with beef, chicken, egg, seaweed, and bean curd, either singularly or in various combinations. This noodle house knows no limit!

Shimane, who has risen to his current position as chef via less glamorous jobs as dishwasher, vegetable-cutter, and tempura chef, seems to instinctively understand the delicacy and subtlety of proper noodle preparation. He explains the secret: "You have to know your flour—it is very sensitive to water and to heat in the room. The key is trying to get the proper consistency and the same quality every day." Shimane also reveals why the act of slurping

noodles is considered proper: "In Japan it's considered proper because it cools the hot noodle as you take it in your mouth, and it makes it taste better." He giggles, "It's barbarian style, but it's fun!"

His noodles are prepared daily in a beautiful, modern machine which greatly reduces preparation time. He makes 44 pounds of *udon* and *soba* in 40 minutes each, which serves approximately 150 people for each batch. Shimane's feeling for texture and consistency is apparent. He explains that the same hand preparation, involving mixing, rolling, and cutting would take almost two days.

Shimane is also a skilled tempura chef. He carefully uses cottonseed oil, heated to 350° to produce the proper cooking temperature for his delicate tempura. He reveals, "The secret is always keeping the same temperature. Experience teaches you when to put the batter in. You have to test first with a few drops, but you really just have to know when it's right."

The casual, subdued tone at Mifune is just the right atmosphere for this style of eating, in the heart of Japantown. Chef Shimane and the Miwa family have captured the essence of Japanese tempura and noodle cooking.

UDON SUKI

1/4 head hakusai (Chinese cabbage)

1 bunch spinach, cleaned and stemmed

1 bunch green onions

4 shiitake mushrooms (Japanese black mushrooms)

1 package atsu-age (fried bean curd)

1 package kamaboko (fish paste cake)

1/2 cup wakame (seaweed), dried or moist

4 prawns, peeled and deveined

2 chicken breasts, boned

4 clams

Soup Stock:

6 cups bonito fish stock

2/3 cup light soy sauce

2 Tbs. sugar

2 Tbs. mirin (sweet sake)

4 portions udon white flour noodles

Chop hakusai, spinach and green onions into 2″ pieces. Soak dried shiitake mushrooms in water to soften. Slice atsu-age into about 8 pieces. Slice kamaboko into about 10 half-circles.

Arrange all of these ingredients plus wakame, prawns, chicken and clams decoratively on a large platter, ready to cook.

In a large pot (preferably earthenware) at the table over a flame, or at the stove if table cooking is not possible, simmer about 1/2 the soup stock. Add 2 portions of udon noodles. When soup begins to slow boil, add 1/2 of all the other ingredients.

The dish is ready to serve after simmering for 10 minutes. Ladle into individual bowls. Do not overcook. After first serving, repeat cooking instructions with the second half of the soup stock and other ingredients.

Lemon can be squeezed into individual bowls to add a distinctive touch.

Serves 4.

MIRAMONTE

Chef: Udo Nechutnys *Owners: Udo Nechutnys & Edward Platel*

German-born Udo Nechutnys works in his kitchen like a man possessed. In his mind, he knows just the way he wants things to happen, and his entire attention focuses on accomplishing just that.

Nechutnys' experience and development as a chef is classic in its progression. His mother cooked well at home. He apprenticed in Barbizon, France at age seventeen ("It was like being a slave but I learned to adapt to pressure"), and then he worked at Maxim's in Paris ("I worked with expensive raw products like truffles and goose liver for the first time"). But, it was Paul Bocuse, the master chef of France, who was really the turning point in Nechutnys' career.

He first worked in Bocuse's 3-Star restaurant in Lyon and then was sent to Bocuse's Mandarin Restaurant in Hong Kong where he ran the kitchen for two years. After a teaching job at a hotel and restaurant school in Osaka, Japan, Nechutnys, with the help of Bocuse, came to California and opened one of the Napa Valley's first French restaurants, the French-owned, Domaine Chandon. Ultimately, Nechutnys and partner Edward Platel, opened Miramonte to realize his own personal goals as a chef and to develop fine dining in the countryside of Northern California.

One basis for his art is Nechutnys' mastery of classic French sauces made from stocks, all of which are created from the bone of the meat, fowl, game, or fish. He recalls to this day that as a child, "I was always amazed that a liquid could be so tasty." He has blended his finely-honed French technique with the best ingredients California has to offer in an ever-changing *prix fixe* menu which gives customers a chance to experience a combination of tastes.

From a *Soupe de Moules* (Mussel Soup) through an *Aiguellette de Canard Sauce Poivres Verte* (Duck with Green Peppercorns), Nechutnys keeps his eye on everything that happens. He sauces many of his own dishes, after which he carefully places the garnishment for proper balance and contrast. Sometimes he has to crack the whip if a waiter doesn't respond quickly enough to a finished dish. "If I see things going wrong, I can get very upset and start screaming. I want consistency. You have to bring the food out the way you want it. Like a conductor, sometimes the musicians don't play the music exactly the way you desire it," he confesses.

Edward Platel, co-owner of Miramonte, says of Nechutnys, "Udo has enormous talent. He has the innate taste for food, and he can do things spontaneously with quite a bit of ease." Perhaps it was the spartan apprenticeship, or his Oriental experiences, or the training by Bocuse, but Nechutnys clearly has the touch of a master chef.

MUSCAT GRAPE TART

1 lb. white grapes, seeded (preferably muscat)

1 shot glass of cognoc

Pie Crust:

1 cup flour

1/2 cup butter or margarine

A little water and salt

Filling:

1/6 cup butter, softened

1/4 cup sugar

1/4 cup powdered almonds

1 egg, beaten

Meringue (optional)

Remove seeds from the grapes which have been washed and dried. Soak in cognac. Make pie crust.

Line the tart tin with your pie crust. Prick the bottom with a fork so that it doesn't swell up. Bake for 15 minutes in a hot oven.

Meanwhile, cream the softened butter with the sugar to obtain a fluffy mixture, then add the powdered almonds and finally the egg. Fill the pre-baked crust with this filling and put it back in the oven for 10 minutes.

Let the tart cool before garnishing it with the grapes. Cover with meringue, if desired, sprinkle with sugar and brown in the oven.

Serves 4.

NARSAI'S

Owner: Narsai M. David   Dinner Chef: Ted Siegel
Catering Chef: Dennis Clews

Watching Narsai David in action is like watching an octopus. The man is everywhere. Genial host and maitre d', kitchen supervisor, TV personality, gourmet food store owner . . . the roles are endless for this dynamic food entrepreneur. At times intimidating to his staff because of his intensity and quest for perfection, Narsai David represents the quintessential contemporary food man—thinking, moving, and creating, with a precision and thoroughness that is rare.

Narsai David caught the food bug early. He reflects, "I got my first restaurant job right out of high school by chance at a drive-in which needed an assistant to the lunch cook. Little by little, I got more involved in it, but I always said I'd never be in the restaurant business for my lifestyle. After running away from it for several years, I finally came to grips with the fact that I really enjoyed the work. I love people. I love good food and good wine, and all of a sudden I was doing the kinds of things I really enjoyed doing. Once I stopped running away from it, I realized that I took great pleasure from it, and it was easier to put in the hours and deal with the craziness because the satisfaction was so great."

Since 1972, Narsai's has turned into one of the premier Bay Area dining rooms. Nestled in the hills of tiny Kensington (north of Berkeley), Narsai's offers a quiet, subdued atmosphere. The tasteful dining room includes a 1/6 cross-section of a wooden tank, made from virgin forest redwood, which is used as a wall on one side of the dining room. Iron sculptures which adorn the walls were fabricated from rods and castings which hold the tank together.

The menu combines both classic French and Mediterranean influences, some of which reflect Narsai's Assyrian heritage, like *Rack of Lamb Assyrian* or *Les Dolmas Shulamith* (named after his mother). One of the highlights of the restaurant is their *prix fixe* Monday and Tuesday night special dinners which explore different cuisines from around the world. A sampling: Independence Day Gala *(Grilled Quail and East Coast Hot Lobster Salad),* Flavors of Hungary *(Salad of Smoked Goose Breast with Melon and Tokay Grapes* and *Medallions of Beef with Tarragon and Sour Cream)*, or a special Bastille Day dinner. The wine list is an absolute marvel—awesome in its scope and depth.

There seems to be no end to the challenge and to the creating for Narsai David. He comments, "When something appears on the market that's exciting, we buy it first and worry about the price later, if it seems at all reasonable. There are no restrictions on the chef on what he can order. We buy things like fresh Maine lobster, Maryland soft shell crabs, and large fresh, Hawaiian prawns . . . things which just catch our fancy, but we use mostly classic style in our preparation."

The amazing Narsai David sets the tone for his whole organization. His persistence and good cooking sense are the essence of this important outpost in the Bay Area's restaurant scene.

RACK OF LAMB, ASSYRIAN

2 large onions, peeled

2 cloves garlic

$^1/_2$ lemon with peeling

$^1/_2$ tspn. pepper

1 cup pomegranate juice

1 tspn. salt

$^1/_2$ cup red wine

2 tspn. basil leaves

2 lamb racks, each with 8-9 ribs (or 3-4 small New Zealand lamb)
Note: Ask the butcher to remove the flap meat and to French cut the rib bones.

Place all ingredients, except for lamb, in a blender or food processor and purée. Rub this marinade into the racks well and put the remaining marinade over the racks in a shallow glass or enameled pan. Let marinate in refrigerator overnight or at room temperature for 6-8 hours.

Wipe off excess marinade and roast in a 450° oven for 10 minutes for medium rare lamb, longer if you like it done to a greater degree.

Serves 4.

THE PEACOCK

Chef: Baldev Singh   Owner: H.S. Bawa

It's not surprising that the food at The Peacock tastes as good as it does. The kitchen is redolent with aromas of exotic spices intermingling, and the food turns out accordingly—elegant and flavorful.

Owner H.S. Bawa has created a soft, refined atmosphere in what was previously a rundown Victorian. This beautiful setting serves as a backdrop for some superb North Indian cuisine, which is derived primarily from the Frontier Province (now Afghanistan and Pakistan). This particular style of cooking features the *tandoor* oven, a deep, sunken, clay-lined oven used to cook chicken, lamb, and various breads, like *Nan* (a fresh, leavened bread), which was supposedly invented in the days of Genghis Khan.

"The *tandoor* ovens are one of the things that makes our cooking really special because it's one of those things you can't do at home very effectively," explains Bawa. "We use mesquite in our ovens to enhance flavors. The temperatures reach 800-900°, the result being that the juices are sealed right into the meat, which makes it tender and succulent." Before being plunged into the fiery depths of the oven, a dish like *Tandoori Murgh* (chicken) is first marinated in yogurt, coriander, cumin, turmeric, and cloves. The chicken is cooked for 10-15 minutes at these extremely hot temperatures, and the result is a juicy, spicy taste sensation which is incomparable.

When the *tandoor* is not in action, the Peacock's chef, Baldev Singh, who comes from Punjab in India, is equally adept at creating such regional specialties as *Rogan Josh Kashmiri* (highly-seasoned lamb curry) or *Baingan Bharta* (charcoal-baked eggplant cooked with tomatoes and herbs). These dishes arrive, rich with exotic spices and cooked proficiently.

Singh explains his approach to Indian cooking: "There is a myth about Indian food that it is hot and burns your tongue. To make food hot is the easiest thing in the world—all you do is add more chili and cayenne pepper. The secret to our cooking is using the right blend of spices for each dish and retaining the authenticity in the way you make it. But the real key is achieving consistency in the food, day in and day out."

CHICKEN CURRY

1 2½ lb. chicken

1 large onion

½ cup vegetable oil

1 Tbs. cumin seeds

1 tspn. fresh ground ginger

½ tspn. fresh ground garlic

1 stick cinnamon, 3-4″ long

6 pieces cloves

¼ tspn. fresh ground black pepper

¼ tspn. turmeric

1 heaping tspn. ground cumin

6 pieces cardamoms

1 tspn. ground coriander

1 medium tomato, chopped

½ cup yogurt

¾ cup water

Salt to taste

1 tspn. paprika

¼ bunch fresh cilantro, cleaned and chopped

Cut the chicken into six small pieces. Slice the onion finely and brown it on slow fire in the vegetable oil along with cumin seeds. When the onions are golden brown, add ginger, garlic, cinnamon, cloves, black pepper, turmeric, ground cumin, cardamoms, ground coriander, tomato, and yogurt. Cook on slow fire until the oil separates from the blend.

Add the chicken pieces and cook for 3-4 minutes stirring all along.

Add water, salt, and paprika and simmer until the chicken is tender and the sauce is reduced, approximately 10-15 minutes.

Sprinkle cilantro and serve hot.

Serves 3-4.

THE RICE TABLE

Chef: Leonie Samuel-Hool   *Owners: Leonie & Bill Hool*

"I was always taught by my Grandma that cookbooks, like spoons and cups used to measure ingredients, were disgraceful things to have in the kitchen. Cooking can only be learned through 'imagination in taste'," says Leonie Hool, a woman born to a Chinese mother and Indonesian father in Depok, Indonesia. Hool started cooking with her Chinese grandmother when she was eight years old and achieved fame as a cook in her home town of Depok when she was still a teenager. She followed in her father's footsteps by opening her own restaurant when she was 17 years old.

The effervescent Hool now runs a traditional Indonesian restaurant with her American husband, Bill, in downtown San Rafael. The Rice Table offers an authentic *rijstafel* (rice table) which is a combination of the most appealing of the varied Indonesian dishes and displays the exotic spices and flavors so essential to this cuisine. The unfolding of the *rijstafel* with *Sate* (marinated chicken), *Udang Goreng* (shrimp fried in butter and tamarind), *Keri Ayam* (chicken curry), *Semur* (beef cooked in butter, soy, and cloves), *Gado Gado* (Indonesian salad with peanut dressing), and *Sate Manis* (pork cooked in sweet and sour sauce) offers a balance of complimentary sweet, sour, and spicy flavors which highlights Hool's liberal use of important Indonesian spices.

Hools grinds her own fresh spices daily

on a *cobek* (stone mortar) and emphasizes lemon grass (grown in her own green house), tamarind, turmeric, coriander, and chili peppers. "Maybe I'm just old-fashioned or superstitious, but spices seem to lose their power and distinctiveness when sliced by metal blades," she explains. While Hool tends to the spices herself, the rest of the kitchen chores are handled by six other family members, making The Rice Table a true family operation.

Cooking is clearly in Hool's blood. "When I was very young, I wanted to cook more than I wanted toys or dolls, but before I was even allowed to touch uncooked food, I had to learn respect for the many spirits that lived in Grandma's kitchen. I can still picture Grandma sitting in her rocking chair smoking a black Java cigar while she chopped, sliced, mixed, tasted, and ordered her servants around. That kitchen was her kingdom and cooking was as much her religion as church," she reminisces.

An amusing woman with a sparkle in her eye, Hool refers to herself as "The Godmother of Indonesian Cooking". She recollects, "We started this restaurant because I used to invite the whole neighborhood over for big home-cooked meals, and my husband, Bill, who was then a patrolman in San Rafael, told me, 'Honey, we can't afford to keep doing this', so we finally decided to open a restaurant."

GADO-GADO (INDONESIAN SALAD)

1 cup chunky peanut butter

2 tspn. shrimp paste

Juice of 2 cloves fresh garlic, pressed or 1 tspn. garlic granules

1 1/2 tspn. salt

2 Tbs. brown sugar

Juice of 1 lemon or 2 Tbs. white vinegar or 2 Tbs. tamarind juice

2 tspn. crushed dry chili peppers (optional)

2 cups boiling water

5 cups mixed vegetables, chopped (carrots, green beans, white cabbage, etc.)

Fried onions (to taste)

Shrimp chips (to taste)

Mix all ingredients, (except the vegetables, water, fried onions, and shrimp chips) thoroughly, then add water slowly. When the peanut butter and spices are mixed and are the consistency of a thick salad dressing, pour over raw vegetable mixture or those that have been boiled lightly or steamed. Garnish with fried onions and shrimp chips. Sauce can be heated also to make it thicker if desired.

Serves 2-4.

RISTORANTE DA LUCIANO

Chef: Bernardo Oropesa   Owner: Luciano Maggiora

If your notion of "Italian" is red and white checkered tablecloths, strands of garlic hanging from the ceiling, rich tomato-garlic sauces, and a loud, fun-loving atmosphere, then Ristorante da Luciano is going to surprise you. With a strong tradition in Northern Italian Piemontese cooking, owner Luciano Maggiora has created a refined, elegant dining atmosphere which highlights the cuisine that he was born and raised with at home.

Watching Chef Bernardo Oropesa and Luciano work together is like watching a marriage that works well. While Luciano handles the maitre d' chores, Bernardo runs the kitchen with skill and efficiency and turns out many flavorful veal dishes and fresh, perfectly cooked pasta. The result is a synchronicity which blends substance with style. Bernardo's *Brasato al Nebbiolo* is a typical example: A tender, succulent veal chop is topped with a rich sauce made from Italy's noblest red wine grape, Nebbiolo, and the dish resounds with flavor.

Luciano talks about the business and the satisfaction he gets from it: "You have to be born for and love the restaurant business. There's no such thing as just doing it for the money because it's perhaps one of the toughest businesses in the world. What I get out of it is, first, meeting people and learning from them. The other thing is: What is more satisfying than producing something so beautiful, and you know that it tastes just as good as it looks? Take Michaelangelo when he created the Piéta. He chiselled for years and years, but look at what came out. Do you realize the satisfaction the man must have had when he finally finished that thing and looked at it?"

The food presented at Luciano's is a hallmark of typical Piemontese cooking. More cream, butter, and wine are used than tomatoes, oregano, and garlic, which are almost unheard of in Northern Italian cooking. Subsequently, the dishes are more subtle and lighter than their southern counterparts.

Luciano says, "When we fix something, I know it's good because I know what goes into it—the highest quality ingredients that are available, but in the end it's the way you present it. Your eyes pop out it looks so good. And all your senses go to work. Your eyes stimulate your palate. You eat in a beautiful dining room, and the whole thing is just perfect. You feel content."

PICCATA DI VITELLO CON CARCIOFINI

4 slices of veal (from ribeye)

All-purpose flour

5 Tbs. clarified butter

Salt and white pepper to taste

2 sprigs parsley, finely chopped

4 Tbs. dry white wine

1 Tbs. lemon juice, freshly squeezed

4 Tbs. chicken broth

$1/2$ cube sweet butter (at room temperature)

1 artichoke heart (boiled in water containing the juice of $1/2$ lemon)

1 Tbs. capers

Carefully and thoroughly pound the veal until thin and flat, but not broken (approximately $1/8''$ thick and $12''$ in circumference). Flour both sides of veal and shake off the excess.

Use a frying pan large enough for four slices of veal. Pour clarified butter into the pan. Turn up the heat (flame should be strong) and place veal into the pan as the butter begins to sizzle. Brown the pieces of veal very quickly; then remove pan from the heat (and drain all the butter) while leaving veal in it.

Season the slices with salt, pepper and chopped parsley. Add the wine, lemon juice, and chicken broth and cook until the wine has almost evaporated. Finally, add the $1/2$ cube sweet butter and stir continuously until the meat is coated in a creamy, white butter sauce; then remove from the heat so that butter doesn't burn.

Place the slices on a hot entrée dish. Quarter the boiled artichoke heart and place one wedge on top of each slice of veal. Add capers to the butter sauce remaining in the pan and sauté briefly over low heat. Pour the sauce over the veal.

Serves 1.

ROSE ET LEFAVOUR

Chef: Bruce LeFavour   Owners: Bruce LeFavour & Carolyn Rose

Bruce LeFavour is a visionary chef whose imagination and willingness to experiment have led him down a culinary trail which may be unmatched in Northern California. LeFavour's interest in food first developed while biking through France from 3-Star to 3-Star restaurant. However, his fascination and first experiences with actual cooking unfolded back in the United States where he ran The Paragon in Aspen, Colorado for eight years.

Completely seft-taught as a chef, LeFavour learned a lot of the practical and technical aspects about cooking from reading books, particularly Louis Diat's book on French cooking. After his stint in Aspen, LeFavour moved to Ketchum, Idaho where he raised ducks and geese and ran a restaurant in an old stage stop called Robinson Bar Ranch. This all amounts to a rather unconventional background for one of California's most talented and creative chefs.

The turning point in LeFavour's career came in 1981 when he moved to the Napa Valley in California where he met Carolyn Rose, a charming, talented woman who professes to being "a food and wine snob", and they decided to open a restaurant together. "It was Kismet, and you conned me into it," she teases. With Rose's talent in design and floral decoration and LeFavour's fascination with a contemporary approach to classic French cooking, the two were off and running with Napa Valley's newest culinary sensation.

LeFavour's own style emphasizes unique combinations of ingredients prepared in somewhat traditional ways. "I get my ideas at strange times," he says. "Sometimes when I'm driving to or from San Francisco, I'll get an inspiration based on something I've seen in the market or perhaps something I've read about."

Offering a seven-course *prix-fixe* dinner every night is no small task, and it is obviously LeFavour's well-developed imagination and good cooking sense which allow him to face the challenge and to succeed brilliantly. Dishes like *Columbia River Sturgeon with Champagne & Sevruga Malassol Caviar Sauce, Alain Senderens' Lobster with Vanilla Sauce, Bombay Madness, The War of 1905—Filet of Beef Russian Style with Bluefish Tuna Japanese Style, Sauté of Fresh Santa Barbara Prawns with Dill & Pernod,* and *Fresh New Zealand Venison Steak with Vinegar Sauce* display the eclecticism of LeFavour's cooking interest as well as a healthy sense of humor.

In the kitchen, LeFavour works in a methodical, detailed way. His plates are individually-styled and have the look of real artistry. The taste only confirms the vision. "I like trying new things all the time because otherwise it gets stale," he admits candidly. It is this curious, inventive nature which sets him apart. The cornucopia of flavors in the balanced progression of dishes lets you know that there's a serious chef working magic in this kitchen.

FRESHLY SMOKED RABBIT LOIN

Dressing:

1/2 small shallot, chopped

1/2 tspn. Dijon mustard

1 tspn. aged wine vinegar

1 Tbs. French peanut oil

Maple chips or hickory sawdust

Make the dressing by mixing all ingredients together. Clean and wash the greens, if necessary. Dry and reserve. Only a small handful per person will be needed.

To smoke rabbit, use a 9″ cast iron pot with a pyrex top. Success depends on getting the smoker "just right"—not the acrid smoke which comes from the first burning and not the heat without smoke which comes after 1/2 hour. The chips or sawdust go on the bottom and smoking is done on a vegetable steamer rack fitted above. A good vent system is a necessity. The the pot and the vegetable steamer are, in all probability, ruined for other uses.

20-25 minutes before serving, place 1 cup of chips or sawdust (1/2 maple and 1/2 hickory sawdust works well) in the bottom of the smoker with the lid on. Place the smoker on a stove over high heat. When it begins to smoke, lift off the top occasionally to vent the

1 Tbs. butter

2 rabbit loins, boned with fat and sinews removed

Salt & pepper to taste

Baby lettuce, rocket, mâche (salad greens)

Chopped chives (garnish)

acrid smoke. Continue to burn until the smoke smells less acrid and seems lighter—about 10-15 minutes.

Melt the butter and roll the loins in it. Salt and pepper to taste and place them on the rack in the smoker. While they are smoking, arrange on the upper left of four warm salad plates the salad which has been tossed in just enough dressing to coat the greens and make them glisten. Do not overdress.

Divide the rest of the dressing into four small pools on the lower right of each plate. The loins are done when they just begin to stiffen, about 3 minutes depending of the intensity of the heat. They should be lightly pink inside.

Slice each loin into 6 or 8 pieces, divide between the plates on the pool of dressing. Sprinkle chopped chives on top and serve.

Serves 4.

SCHROEDER'S

Chef: Manfred Oeltze   Owner: Max Kniesche

Walk into historic Schroeder's German Restaurant in downtown San Francisco, and you find a cross between an old Bavarian beer hall and a chummy men's lunch club. Schroeder's has been a San Francisco institution since 1893 when its doors first opened, and it has stood steadfastly through location and ownership changes over the years. The Max Kniesche family has presided over the restaurant since 1922, and the current version reflects the strong German heritage of all of its owners.

Murals of beer-drinking revelry adorn the walls. A beautiful mahogany rosewood bar serves as headquarters for beer sampling, while diners read about the daily specials from blackboards and eat on polished oak tables. Tuxedoed waiters round out the authentic German atmosphere.

Not surprisingly, the food reflects the environment at Schroeder's. It is a proud display of old-style German cooking with no pretenses or fanfare. This is hearty, soul-satisfying food—the kind you'd imagine having in a German hofbrau on a rainy day.

The kitchen bustles with activity, particularly during the hectic Financial District lunch hour. Chef Manfred Oeltze presides over his briskets, *Sauerbraten*, sausages, and ribs like a dignified German Chancellor. These dishes, embellished with other typical German specialties like potato pancakes and sauerkraut, roll out with speed and precision.

Chef Oeltze, who apprenticed in Berlin and has worked at the Banff Springs Hotel, the Mark Hopkins Hotel, and the Iron Horse, approaches his job as a challenge. He elaborates, "As a chef you have to travel around because you learn new things everywhere you go. Here it's a matter of perfecting my own system and establishing consistency with dishes like *Sauerbraten*, which may have been a family recipe before I was even born. People come to a place like this because they find dishes they like and want to capture that same taste over and over again. That's what I aim to give them."

SAUERBRATEN

2 cups vinegar

4 cups water

1 large onion, diced

1/4 cup whole mixed spices

Salt to taste

5 lbs. beef (rump or top round)

2 Tbs. shortening

3 Tbs. flour

2 Tbs. sugar

1/2 glass red wine

Make a pickling solution of the vinegar, water, onions, spices, and a little salt; soak the meat in it for two to three days, turning frequently. At the end of the time, remove the meat from the solution and place in the hot fat, browning it on all sides. Remove to tray or plate. Brown flour in the fat. Add spices from the pickling solution, a little water, sugar, and simmer a few minutes.

Place the browned meat in a roasting pan, add the sauce, cover pan and bake the meat from 2 1/2 to 3 hours in 350° oven. Turn and baste frequently. One half hour before the meat is done, add the red wine.

When done, lift meat to hot platter, add water and flour paste to make gravy, straining it into a gravy boat. If sauce is not sour enough, add a little vinegar and mix into it.

Serves 6.

SQUARE ONE
Chef: Joyce Esersky Goldstein

Joyce Goldstein's obsession with food and cooking is so pervasive that opening her own restaurant is the only thing she really could do to keep herself happy. For someone who considered food to be "an ordeal" as a child, Goldstein has blossomed into one of the Bay Area's most important teachers and chefs.

Formerly a landscape painter, Goldstein started cooking in college because "it provided instant gratification and brought people into my life". By the mid-1970's, cooking had taken over, and she opened the California Street Cooking School. She also wrote a cookbook called *Feedback*, (Richard Marek, $10.95) which dealt with cooking as a meditative and spiritual experience as well as offering a plentiful choice of her favorite recipes. Ultimately, Goldstein wound up managing the kitchen at the Cafe at Chez Panisse where she developed her skills as a kitchen organizer as well as a restaurant chef for the first time ("I started with pasta and pizza dough, and I discovered that I loved it!")

Goldstein is a vibrant, energetic woman, and has totally immersed herself in the plans for her new restaurant, Square One, which will open in mid-1984. She specializes in kitchen layout and design and seems as comfortable skimming a set of blueprints as she does with a recipe book. She also scouts local auction houses for good deals on equipment to use in the new restaurant.

As a chef, Goldstein has assimilated many different styles and has blended them into what can loosely be called "Mediterranean style". "I'm a classicist," she says. "If I get interested in a cuisine of a certain country, I research it like a maniac and then try to define it through my own palate. At Square One, we'll do Greek, Turkish, Lebanese, Moroccan, Syrian, and even some Brazilian dishes, but Italian and Middle Eastern dishes are my passions," she confesses.

"Mediterranean food is very sensual. It has wonderful flavors and textures, and it's not glopped up with sauces. It's distinctive and robust, not ethereal and delicate. I have this immense recipe file which spins in my head, and I'm quite excited about sharing it."

As she emphasizes in her book, cooking is a dynamic exercise: "I want people to feel like they're coming to my house and having me cook for them. Cooking is energizing for me. The manual and physical parts of it are really stimulating. If I don't cook every day, I find I'm depressed. Cooking is what keeps me grounded and straight. It's making the food that means everything to me. If I didn't make some dish every day, I'd feel deprived. Life would be a waste of time."

COUSCOUS

2-2 1/2 lbs. lean lamb in 1 1/2 " cubes (shoulder is best)

6-8 Tbs. oil or butter

1 3/4 tspn. salt

2 1/4 tspn. black pepper (or 1/2 tspn. black, 1/2 tspn. cayenne

1 1/4 tspn. ginger

3/4 tspn. saffron

1 1/4 tspn. paprika

1 1/4 tspn. cinnamon

Peel of lemon

2 onions, cut in chunks

3 cups cold water or lamb stock

3-4 carrots, 2 " lengths

2-3 turnips, peeled and chunked

1/2 cup raisins

15 1/2 oz. can chick-peas or 1 cup dry chick-peas, soaked overnight

3-4 zucchini, 2 " lengths

1 lb. couscous

2 cups water

Salt to taste

4 Tbs. butter

1 tspn. cinnamon

Marinate lamb in a small amount of oil with 1/4 tspn. each of salt, pepper, ginger, saffron, paprika, and cinnamon, plus lemon peel for several hours.

In a heavy kettle, sauté the lamb until brown in approximately 5 Tbs. butter or oil, or a combination of both. Set aside.

Sauté onions in 2-3 Tbs. butter or oil until soft. Add the remaining amount of spices and cook for a few minutes. Add lamb and water or lamb stock, then simmer for 1/2 hour. Add carrots and cook for 15 minutes. Add turnips and cook for 15 minutes more. Then add raisins, chick-peas, and zucchini and cook for 7 additional minutes. Add salt and pepper to taste. Keep warm.

Cook couscous in lightly salted water, butter, and cinnamon and cook for 5 minutes. Separate grains by rubbing between hands or sift through a strainer.

Mound couscous on a platter. Surround with meat and vegetables.

Serves 6.

TADICH GRILL

Chef: John Canepa   Owners: Steve, Robert, & Mary Buich

The Tadich Grill is a venerable San Francisco restaurant which dates back to the Gold Rush days of 1849. Tadich's has survived a series of changes in location and still serves some of the best, freshest seafood in town. The restaurant is currently owned by the Buich family who bought it from John Tadich in 1928. Tadich Grill has that old San Francisco feeling with high ceilings, wood paneling, a long counter, which is always busy and interesting, and private booths for those looking for a little quiet.

The food at Tadich's is simplicity itself—fresh, understated, and consistent. Chef John Canepa and his assistants turn out a variety of fresh fish dishes which are available charcoal-broiled, poached, pan-fried, sautéed, deep-fried, or baked. The action is fast in the kitchen, and watching Canepa and his staff cook is like seeing a well-oiled piece of machinery—all the parts seem to be synchronous.

"The secret to preparing fish properly is getting fish with good firmness; glossy and moist in appearance," Canepa advises.

"I like to sauté dry, lightly floured fish in half butter and half oil quickly over medium temperature, but never overcook the fish. You can use herbs and glaze with white wine. For broiling, you must start with a clean grill. The temperature must be hot, and broiling should be done quickly to retain moisture."

Chef Canepa's background obviously influences his cooking philosophy: "My father was a chef in the East European tradition. He taught me to have pride in my product and to express this pride through the quality of what I cook. My cooking is very clean and precise. I use only fresh, natural foods and ingredients. I want to satisfy the customer 100%. When a customer comes in he can see what he is eating. I never disguise the food or cloud it in an overbearing sauce. I like to highlight the natural, fresh flavor of the product and present it in an appealing manner. It is very easy for me as a chef to create what I like, but I am primarily motivated by what the customer enjoys and wants."

SCALLOPS SAUTÉ A LA CANEPA

18 medium scallops

1 Tbs. flour

2 Tbs. olive oil

4 oz. butter

3 Tbs. chopped onion

Salt, cayenne pepper, and nutmeg (to taste)

2 oz. chardonnay or chablis

6 oz. whipping cream

1/2 cup sour cream

1 Tbs. chives

1 tspn. chopped parsley

Juice from 1 lemon

Drain scallops. Dust well with flour.

In sauté skillet, heat oil and 2 oz. butter to medium temperature. Add scallops, cooking and turning them until lightly browned. Add chopped onion, salt, cayenne pepper, and nutmeg; cook and stir for 2 minutes. Add wine and cook to reduce wine. Add whipping cream and cook for 4 minutes. Remove from heat.

Stir in sour cream, chives, chopped parsley, 2 oz. solid butter, and lemon juice.

Serve immediately with buttered noodles and vegetables.

Serves 2.

TOMMASO'S

Chefs: Maria & Lydia Crotti   *Owner: Agostino Crotti*

San Francisco's most famous and best pizzeria is Tommaso's, a North Beach legend, which is run by the Crotti family. While pizza is king at Tommaso's, the Crottis serve a wide array of Neapolitan specialties out of an oak-burning brick oven which reaches temperatures of 700°.

Sitting in Tommaso's, it's easy to harken back to the past. The walls are lined with faded murals of Italian scenes, and the whole restaurant is permeated with a certain kind of warmth that you'd expect to find in a little, tucked-away *trattoria* outside Naples. Tommaso's actually derives both its location and menu from what used to be called Lupo's, a famous North Beach restaurant which dates back 50 years. The oven itself could probably tell tales for days.

At the heart of the home-spun atmosphere is Maria Crotti, a hard-working, middle-aged woman who exudes all the good qualities of Italian mothers. Maria Crotti is typically humble and unassuming about her role in the kitchen: "The secret is good ingredients and simply-prepared homemade cooking in the wood oven. The oak oven is the only way they cook pizza in Italy, and it gives our pizza that authentic flavor and good crust."

Beyond the tempting *Pizzas*, which are available in nineteen variations, Mrs. Crotti makes a succulent *Calzone*, which is folded pizza dough filled with ricotta and mozzarella cheese, prosciutto ham, and spices. Cooked in the wood oven to a crispy finish, it takes on magical qualities. The Crotti's also cook fresh seafood dishes, like *Coo Coo Clams*, in the same oven. The heat of the oven (even in the cooler section away from the wood) cooks the clams fast and leaves the freshness and moisture intact.

Maria Crotti is typical of the old-style chef who is relying on tradition and a straight-forward approach to cooking to satisfy her customers. She seems to revel in the simple, tactile stuffing of the *Calzone* . . . her hands caressing the ingredients and the dough. Then, as she reaches into the hot oven for the finished dish, she sees she has captured it at just the right moment.

She says of her cooking, "I cook because people enjoy it, and that makes me feel real good. They come and tell me 'Thank you for the wonderful pizza, like Mama-style', because I'm Mama here. Everyone calls me that."

BAKED COO-COO CLAMS

24 fresh clams

1/2 tspn. dry oregano

1/2 tspn. basil

12 Tbs. oil

6 Tbs. red wine vinegar

Minced garlic (to taste)

1/4 tspn. crushed chili pepper (to taste)

Salt and pepper (to taste)

In a small frying pan, combine all ingredients and bake at 450° until the clams open well.

Serves 2-3.

TON KIANG

Chef: Willie Seam   *Owners: The Wong Family*

Of the 4300 restaurants in San Francisco, a large percentage of them are Chinese. But nowhere do you see people standing in the rain on a wet, winter night for 45 minutes waiting to eat except at Ton Kiang. Throngs of hungry diners regularly flock to this Hakka Chinese restaurant to sample the savory, unusual cuisine.

Originally from the northern part of China, the Hakka people were forced out by Manchurian invaders who drove them to other areas of China, particularly near Canton. These poor, nomadic people developed a cuisine based on simple, inexpensive ingredients which could be easily preserved.

The Wongs, a Hakka family from China, have opened three restaurants in San Francisco dedicated to preparing these regional Hakka specialties. Chef Willie Seam, who was trained in Hong Kong, runs the kitchen at the Ton Kiang on Geary and 22nd Avenue with skill and efficiency. Seam and his staff are masters of the traditional Chinese stir-frying technique, but they also specialize in many wine-flavored dishes which are cooked in clay pot.

It is Seam's good, basic cooking sense and speed which have earned him his reputation and following. Seam observes,

"We cook really simple food. With the clay pot dishes, we usually marinate first, then stir-fry, and finally we boil the dish in a clay pot in a special wine-flavored sauce using sweet rice wine that we make ourselves. This helps develop a complexity of flavors."

Seam also applies traditional Hakka food preservation techniques to ingredients like mustard greens and pickles which are then used in dishes such as *Sliced Pork with Dry Mustard Greens. Salt-Baked Chicken* is an old-style Hakka specialty which traditionally used rock salt while baking the chicken. The key to the dish, however, is moving it from hot to cold water after the baking to help retain moisture and juiciness in the chicken. There are also Hakka dishes which integrate steamed or braised meat stuffed in bean curd.

Claiming to cook because "it was all I could do since my English isn't very good", Seam is obviously a master of the craft. His whole kitchen buzzes at a feverish pace as the various time-consuming phases of preparation are done. Smells, flavors, and textures merge together as part of a greater whole in this exciting addition to the varied world of Chinese food.

MIXED SEAFOOD IN TARO ROOT BASKET

1/2 cup taro root

Salt and pepper to taste

1/4 Tbs. cornstarch

Vegetable oil

8 scallops

3 prawns, shelled and deveined

8 pieces squid, cleaned

4 pieces baby corn

5 pieces sliced bamboo shoots

8 straw mushrooms

5 sliced water chestnuts

1/8 cup chopped celery

1/8 cup green peas

1/8 cup julienned carrot

2 Tbs. sesame oil (for stir-frying)

1/4 Tbs. sugar

2 tspn. soy sauce

Skin, shred, and wash taro root. Add a small amount of salt and cornstarch and mix throughly. Drain and dry taro root. In a 6″ strainer, line the inside with the taro root mixture. Place another strainer inside the first one to keep the mixture in place. Press down slightly. Place strainers in a large pot of boiling vegetable oil and cook for 3 minutes under reduced heat or until taro root is slightly browned. Knock basket out of strainer into oil and continue cooking for another minute.

Place fish in a strainer in a wok filled with boiling water for 1 minute. Add baby corn, bamboo shoots, mushrooms, water chestnuts, celery, green peas and carrots and continue cooking for 30 seconds to 1 minute. Place entire mixture in a large pot of water for less than a minute.

In a hot wok, stir fry mixture in sesame oil, sugar and soy sauce for 1-2 minutes. Pour into taro root basket and serve.

Note: Exact amounts of ingredients for fish are not critical. Likewise cooking times may vary according to flame.

Serves 1-2.

RENÉ VERDON'S LE TRIANON

Chef:René Verdon   *Owners: René & Yvette Verdon*

If ever someone was born to be a chef, there's a good chance René Verdon would be that person. Born to a French family which was heavily involved in cooking, Verdon chose his profession, or perhaps it chose him, shortly after finishing his schooling. He describes his introduction to cooking: "I think my motivation to cook started when I was a little kid, maybe ten or twelve. But later on after my school, my father asked me what I wanted to do. We had one pastry chef and one baker in the family already. He said, 'Why don't you become a chef and complete the trio?'. I decided that I loved cooking then, and I still love it now."

René Verdon's Le Trianon is a testament to that love. It is arguably the head-quarters for *haute cuisine* in San Francisco, and if you ever wondered where to find beautifully-prepared dishes with exquisite, rich sauces, this is the place. The atmosphere in the dining room is elegant, subdued, and relaxed, while in the kitchen Verdon works his magic with a dedication and commitment to quality which is unparalleled.

He outlines his background which led to the development of Le Trianon: "In '58, I was already a chef in Europe, but I decided to go to New York to work. Soon after I arrived there, I had an opportunity to work for the Kennedy family in the White House. The Secret Service came in and checked on my past, and finally I was accepted. The White House . . . that experience was wonderful because I was like family with them. Wherever the President and First Lady would go, I would go with them—Palm Beach, Newport, Camp David, all over. So, the White House was like a family restaurant and a big hotel. We had different groups to prepare for—breakfast for the children, then a banquet, and two or three small parties going on. It was something!"

Verdon followed his White House stint by going on the road for a big cooking manufacturer. There he met his wife, Yvette, and they decided to buy Le Trianon, which was on the skids at the time. He quickly turned things around with his solid approach to classic cooking. "It's the wish of any chef to open his own restaurant, and then, after you do, you know what kind of trouble you are really into," he explains.

"I always cook fresh. I am not an adventurous person like some people who are serving *nouvelle cuisine*. I don't believe in that. Everything is based on the old cuisine. I follow the evolution in Europe to get ideas for new dishes. But mostly, I look for freshness."

In fact, there are some newer dishes offered at Le Trianon. Verdon experiments occasionally with dishes like lamb with sweet garlic. He also uses poussin and specially-raised ducks, but it is the traditional dishes at Le Trianon which are the real magic—*Quenelles de Faisan* or his unequaled *Grand Marnier Soufflé*, which defines the state-of-the-art with its well-conceived flavors and ethereal texture.

Verdon confesses, "Cooking is something that's in my blood, I guess. Sometimes the problems get to me, but I still love it."

MOUSSELINE ST. JACQUES

14 oz. fresh scallops (Coquilles St. Jacques)

1 whole egg

1 egg white

Salt, pepper, and nutmeg to taste

1/2 quart heavy cream

1/2 Tbs. chopped truffles (optional)

1 oz. melted butter

Sauce:

1 tspn. very finely chopped shallots

2 Tbs. vinegar

1/2 cup Muscadet wine (Wine from the Loire area)

1/4 cup heavy cream

1/4 lb. salted butter

1/4 lb. sweet butter

Salt and white pepper to taste

Garnishing:

1 bunch fresh spinach, shredded

1 bunch watercress, shredded

1 Tbs. butter

Grind the scallops using the fine blade of a meat grinder, then cool for 1/2 hour in refrigerator. Place the scallops, egg, egg white, salt, pepper, and nutmeg in a food processor and run for 1 minute. Add the cream by pouring it through the opening at the top for 3 seconds until blended. Add truffles, if used. (Be careful not to overblend as it will become buttery.)

Butter a 6″ to 8″ mold with melted butter and pour in mixture. Bake mold in shallow pan containing 1″ of water; cover the pan with aluminum foil and cook for 30 minutes at 350°.

To make sauce, place shallots, vinegar, and wine into a small saucepan and reduce until half the liquid is gone. Add cream and bring to a boil. Add the butter in small pieces and melt by swirling the pan over the heat; then remove pan from heat. Salt and pepper to taste.

Sauté the raw spinach and watercress in 1 Tbs. butter for 1 minute *al dente*.

On individual hot serving plates, lay a little of the spinach and watercress mixture in a circle the same size as the mold. Unmold the scallop mousse on the above mixture. Pour the sauce over all and serve.

Serves 8.

VIVANDE PORTA VIA
Chef & Owner: Carlo Middione

The last of thirteen children, Carlo Middione's fate in life was to be a chef. Middione's autocratic father, who was a fine chef himself, wanted his youngest son to be either a chef or a priest. Although Middione approaches his craft with almost religious fervor, it's clear that the decision to cook was the right one since he has the natural talent and dedication found amongst only the most successful chefs.

Vivande is Middione's personal contribution to San Francisco's varied culinary world. It is both a restaurant and a food market in the tradition of Fauchon in Paris or Peck's in Milan, and the stunning array of freshly-cooked pastas, breads, pastries, sausages, pizzas, and various *antipasti* are so mouth-wateringly displayed that only the strong-willed can restrain themselves. It's a food lover's paradise, designed to tempt and titillate the eye and the palate.

Carlo Middione is a pragmatic, earthy man whose joy in his profession is evident constantly: "Cooks are driven to do what they do, and you have to have an uncontrollable drive. I'm interested in any dish that looks and tastes good regardless of what region it's from. I'm more interested in re-creating than creating. I'm a good craftsman, and I don't mind the repetition. There's a lot of great creative chefs around, but I'm personally not interested in ceremonial eating or pretension. I get more excited by things like a perfect case of tomatoes than by Beluga caviar or more exotic ingredients."

Vivande's open kitchen is a classic of function and efficiency. Everyone and everything seems orgainzed in order to accommodate the wide range of cooking which includes spit-roasting, baking, braising, frying, and sautéing. From one end of the kitchen to the other, you can absorb the smells of fresh garlic and basil, chocolate and butter, and freshly baked bread.

Utilizing a smoke oven which burns alder, applewood, or fresh mesquite to slowly cook chicken, turkey, duck, sausages, and shrimp, Middione's smoked chicken is so succulent and flavorful that you could swear a half dozen seasonings were used, yet it's simply the natural flavor of smoked chicken which explodes on your palate.

Middione seems to instinctively understand the direct relationship between the cooking process at Vivande and his patrons: "Our food has the stamp of individuality—it's not bulk-processed food. We work in full view of our patrons, and I think that gives them a sense of security and involvement. Some of the world's finest chefs are stuck in basement kitchens completely out of touch with their customers. I like seeing a person's involvement with my food and getting that kind of instant feedback between the performance and the reaction."

Despite the difficulty of the job, Middione approaches it with a sense of wonderment. "The true creativity or greatness of cooking comes when you least expect it," he says. "You cook every day, and no matter what you feel like, you always have to be ready . . . the show must go on! But sometimes, like when I'm baking a loaf of fresh bread, I'll have a great moment and feel absolutely triumphant. That's what makes it for me."

SPAGHETTI ALLA PUTTANESCA (HOOKER'S PASTA)

2-3 Tbs. olive oil

2 garlic cloves, minced

2 oz. or more Calamata black olives, pitted and coarsely chopped

1 tspn. capers, coarsely chopped

1 large fresh tomato, peeled and coarsely chopped

4-5 anchovy fillets, coarsely chopped

1 pound spaghetti

$^1/_3$ cup parsley, finely chopped

Salt and pepper (to taste)

Red pepper flakes (optional)

Place the olive oil in a frying pan and add the minced garlic. When it is golden, add the olives, capers, tomato, and anchovy fillets. Stir well and heat through for about 6 minutes.

Cook the pasta *al dente* and drain it. Place in a warm bowl and add half the sauce. Toss well. Add the remaining sauce and sprinkle on the parsley with some salt and pepper to taste. Serve hot.

There is no cheese used with this dish. It can also be eaten later cold.

Optional: Sprinkle red pepper flakes over the top before serving.

Serves 4-6.

XENIOS

Chef: Theo Bouhoutsos   Owner: Peter Stavros

If your notion of Greek restaurants is a small, crowded room with belly-dancers and Greek music blasting out of tinny speakers, then the refined, elegant atmosphere of the Stavros family's Xenios is going to surprise you. Greek restaurants are a tradition with the Stavros'—Jim and Stella Stavros started the first Greek restaurant in California, the Golden Peacock, which was one of San Francisco's finest years ago. Their son, Peter, now runs Xenios, which maintains the tradition and the recipes of his parents' restaurant.

Young Stavros has placed the emphasis on traditional Greek dishes like *Mousaka* (eggplant casserole), *Dolmades* (stuffed grape leaves), and *Souvlakia* (broiled lamb kebabs), but he also integrates some newer Greek and Mediterranean specialties. To head the kitchen at Xenios, Stavros hired Theo Bouhoutsos, one of the better chefs from Athens. Stavros comments on Bouhoutsos' abilities, "All great chefs have pride in themselves. Theo's great accomplishment is that he cooks as consistently for two hundred as he does for five, and he has great instincts in the kitchen."

Greek cuisine is likely to fall into different categories, depending on the region. In the North, dishes can be a little heavier, whereas in the warmer South, chefs cut down on fats and oils and dishes are more lightly spiced. Bouhoutsos tends toward the Southern-style, and his talent can be easily recognized in the signature dish, *Mousaka*. "*Mousaka* is a very simple dish, and it can be done many different ways. You can do it with eggplant, zucchini, or potato, or a combination. You can use ground lamb or beef. But you always need a good *béchamel*. You must drain the eggplant and use careful preparation and good, fresh cooking technique," Bouhoutsos advises.

The kitchen at Xenios seems to be a family affair—Peter handles overall management; Bouhoutsos prepares entrées while his assistant, Khosrow Radji handles sauces and pastries; but, the real life-blood and spirit comes from Mama Stella Stavros, who makes sure that the family recipes are being followed properly. Mama Stella, like all good mothers, offers a morsel of *Spanikopita* (a Greek spinach and cheese pie). "Taste this . . . you'll love it!" she exclaims. Mama Stella radiates warmth and pride as she shows off her *Vlahiko* (lamb, vegetables, and cheese wrapped in dough).

Xenios, with its modern mirrored look, may at first seem out of character for such traditional food, but the surroundings only serve to focus attention on the subtle seasonings and dedicated preparation of one of the world's oldest cuisines.

MOUSAKA

4 large eggplants
1 cup olive oil
2 large onions, diced
2 lbs. ground lamb
1/2 bunch parsley, chopped
2 Tbs. tomato paste or 2 large tomatoes
2 Tbs. salt

1 Tbs. black pepper
1 Tbs. mint, chopped
6 eggs, beaten
1 cup parmesan cheese
1 quart milk
4 Tbs. butter
2 Tbs. corn starch

Slice the eggplant lengthwise at 4 slices per eggplant. Remove skin (optional). Fry or bake in oil until browned. Place cooked eggplant on paper towel to absorb excess oil. Set aside.

In deep frying pan, heat oil. Fry onions until limp and brown. Add ground lamb, parsley, tomato paste or tomatoes, salt, pepper, and mint. Simmer together uncovered for 20 minutes. Remove pan from heat. Add 3 eggs and 1/4 cup parmesan cheese to mixture and blend together well.

In a separate pan, bring 3 cups milk and butter to a boil. Dissolve corn starch in the remaining cup of cold milk. Add to heated milk. Stir in well and remove from heat when mixture begins to thicken. Add 1/4 cup of parmesan and remaining eggs to milk mixture. Stir well.

Line the bottom of a 10" × 14" × 4" pan with fried eggplant slices. Spread with lamb mixture evenly over eggplant. Cover with another layer of eggplant. Pour milk and eggs mixture evenly over entire surface of eggplant. Sprinkle with remaining parmesan cheese.

Bake in a 350° to 400° preheated oven for 15 to 20 minutes covered with foil. Remove foil and cook until top is golden brown. Serve hot.

Serves 8-12.

ZOLA'S

Chef: Catherine Pantsios   *Owners: Catherine Pantsios & Larry Bain*

While some chefs utilize a vivid imagination and free association to create their dishes, young Catherine Pantsios' cooking is primarily rooted in history and tradition as a source of inspiration for her dishes. As evidenced by the name of her restaurant, Zola's (named after 19th Century novelist, Emile Zola), Pantsios enjoys delving into the history of France and its culinary traditions to "re-invent" new dishes which echo the past. Yet, her cooking comes across as new, fresh, and exciting. What is this magical connection?

Catherine Pantsios, unlike many top chefs, did not grow up in a food family, surrounded by years of tradition of cooking. Her interest in food is strictly personal. "I remember loving cream puffs as a kid and wanting to learn how to make them," she reminisces. Pantsios' road to Zola's is marked with stops along the way in a high school cafeteria ("That taught me how to deal with volume and to get organized mentally and spatially"), then at the Ritz-Carlton Hotel in Chicago, and at The Seventh Inn in Boston ("My teacher, Hiroshi Hayashi, taught us obedience and discipline in the kitchen"), and finally at the Hayes Street Grill in San Francisco ("I learned a great deal about the grill as a heat source").

In the meantime, she travelled in Italy and France, getting a healthy dose of training and inspiration in French provincial and Northern Italian cooking. "*Haute cuisine* is traditionally men's cooking, and it's almost impossible for a woman to break in. Regional cooking is the kind women do," she explains.

Zola's, which opened in February 1983, is the culmination of Pantsios' somewhat eclectic past. The menu, however, travels straight down a French country road. *Endive Salad with Tongue Confit and Pears* uses traditional meat preservation techniques from Southwest France in combination with unusual ingredients. *Lamb Stew with White Beans* is a fragrant mixture of lamb, white beans, thyme, orange peel, and garlic, which echoes a cold winter night in a French country inn. Her *Tomato Tart* could appear in a summer picnic lunch basket.

Pantsios is clear and pragmatic about her cooking goals: "Any style of cooking has to have some kind of logic. It might be based on history or on the logical relationship of ingredients to their environment. My cooking has to make sense to me. I'm interested in variations on classic things which have a solid basis, like a mathematical equation which is economical in its expression. People don't always want to be startled by a dish. They like to be soothed and comforted by food too. The food should be supportive to the whole dining experience."

TOMATO TART

Dough:

1 cup warm water

2 Tbs. dry yeast

2 Tbs. olive oil

1 Tbs. kosher salt

3 cups all-purpose flour

12 ripe red or yellow plum tomatoes

Salt & pepper to taste

Virgin olive oil to taste

6 tspn. fresh rosemary, chopped

6 tspn. fresh oregano, chopped

To make dough, blend water, yeast, olive oil and salt until mixed. Add flour, one cup at a time, and process after each addition. Process until mixture balls up. Knead for a minute by hand, and then divide into 2 oz. balls. Let rise for about an hour, then roll out into circles, approximately 5" in diameter.

To make tarts, slice the tomatoes (they must be ripe, preferably in the summer) and arrange on dough in one layer. Sprinkle with salt and pepper, drizzle with virgin olive oil and herbs. One tomato and 1/2 tspn. each of the herbs should be used per individual tart. Bake on a baking sheet in preheated 500° oven until the edges of dough are brown and crisp (about 5-10 minutes, depending on oven).

Makes 12 pieces.

APPENDIX
List of Restaurants: Pertinent Data

ALEJANDRO'S SOCIEDAD GASTRONÓMICA
1840 Clement St.
San Francisco, CA 94121
(415) 668-1184
Open 7 days a week; 5 PM - 11 PM
Reservations Suggested
Corkage: $4.00 Wine; $5.00 Champagne
Tapas (Appetizer Bar) on Friday, Saturday, and
Sunday
Visa, MC, AX, DC, CB

BUREAU OF FISH & GAME
To be announced mid-'84
San Francisco, CA
No data yet available

CAFE ROYALE
2080 Van Ness Ave. (at Pacific)
San Francisco, CA 94109
(415) 441-1300
Open 7 days a week: Bar opens at 5 PM; Dinner
6 PM until midnight
Reservations Recommended
Corkage: $5.00 Wine; $10.00 Champagne
Valet Parking; Piano Entertainment Nightly
Visa, MC, AX

CALIFORNIA CULINARY ACADEMY
215 Fremont St.
San Francisco, CA 94105
(415) 546-1316
Open Mondays-Friday, Lunch (12:20 PM), Dinner (6, 6:30, 7:00 PM)
Reservations for Monday-Wednesday required 2
days in advance; Thursday and Friday required
2 weeks in advance.
Corkage: $5.00, however restaurant has exten-
sive, reasonably priced wine list.
Grand Classical European buffets at lunch Fri-
days and dinner Thursday and Friday; Private
parties (minimum 150) can book the entire room.
Visa, MC, AX

CAMPTON PLACE HOTEL
340 Stockton St.
San Francisco, CA 94108
(415) 781-5155
Open 7 days a week; 7-11 AM Breakfast;
11:30-2:30 PM Lunch; 6-10 PM Dinner
Reservations Necessary
Corkage: $10.00
Brunch on Sundays
All major credit cards

LE CASTEL
3235 Sacramento St.
San Francisco, CA 94118
(415) 921-7115
Open Monday-Saturday; 6-10 PM
Reservations Recommended
Corkage: $7.50
AX, MC, Visa, Diners

CHEZ PANISSE
1517 Shattuck Ave.
Berkeley, CA 94709
(415) 548-5525
Open Tuesday-Saturday; Seatings at 6, 6:30, 8:30,
9 PM; Cafe open Monday-Saturday 11 AM-11 PM
Reservations Required for restaurant; No reser-
vations in Cafe
Corkage: $10.00
Zinfandel Festival featuring Nouveau Zinfandel,
Garlic Festival, seasonal Fall menus
No credit cards; Cash and personal checks only

CHINA MOON
393 Hayes
San Francisco, CA 94102
(415) 863-MOON
Open Tuesday-Saturday; 11:30 AM-12 Midnight
Reservations Accepted
Corkage: $6.00
Yearly China Moon Festival, featuring foods of
individual provinces
MC, Visa

COQUELICOT
23 Ross Common
Ross, CA 94957
(415) 461-4782
Open for lunch Tuesday-Friday, 11:30-2:00; din-
ner Tuesday-Saturday 6-10 PM
Reservations Recommended
Corkage: $8.00 Wine; $10.00 Champagne
Visa, MC

ELITE CAFE
2049 Fillmore St.
San Francisco, CA 94115
(415) 346-8668
Open Monday-Saturday 5-11 PM; Sunday 10-3
PM, 5-10 PM
No reservations
Corkage: $5.00
No credit cards

ERNIE'S
847 Montgomery St.
San Francisco, CA 94133
(415) 397-5969
Open 7 days a week; 6-11 PM
Reservations Required
Corkage: $15.00
Special 50th Anniversary menus
All major credit cards

FOURTH STREET GRILL
1820 Fourth St.
Berkeley, CA 94710
(415) 849-0526
Open 7 days a week; 11:30-2:30 PM, 5:30-10 PM
No reservations
Corkage: $6.00
Regional menus on weekends monthly
MC, Visa

APPENDIX
List of Restaurants: Pertinent Data

GEORGE'S SPECIALTIES
3420 Balboa
San Francisco, CA 94121
(415) 752-4009
Open Tuesday-Saturday 6-9 PM
Reservations Accepted
Corkage: $5.00
Visa, MC, Diners

GERTIE'S CHESAPEKE BAY CAFE
1919 Addison St.
Berkeley, CA 94704
(415) 841-CRAB
Open Tuesday-Saturdays, 11 AM-11 PM, Sunday
10:30 AM-10 PM
Reservations Accepted
Corkage: $3.00
Sunday Dixieland Brunch
Visa, MC, AX

GOLDEN TURTLE
308 5th Ave.
San Francisco, CA 94118
(415) 221-5285
Open Tuesday-Friday, 5 PM-10:30 PM, Saturdays
& Sundays, 11 AM-11 PM
Reservations Accepted before 7 PM
Corkage: Not Acceptable
Visa, MC, AX

GREENS AT FORT MASON
Building A - Fort Mason
San Francisco, CA 94123
(415) 771-6222
Open Tuesday-Saturday, 11:30-2:30; Friday-
Saturday 6-8:30 PM; Sunday Brunch 10-2 PM
Reservations Required up to one week in
advance for lunch; up to 3 months in advance
for dinner
Corkage: $6.00
Special events by arrangement
Visa, MC

GULF COAST OYSTER BAR
736 Washington St.
Oakland, CA 94607
(415) 839-6950
Open Monday-Friday, 11:30-2:30 PM, Tuesday-
Saturday, 5:30-10 PM
Reservations Required at dinners; not at lunch
Corkage: $3.50
Visa, MC

HAYES STREET GRILL
324 Hayes St.
San Francisco, CA 94102
(415) 863-5545
Open Monday-Friday, 11:30-3PM; Monday-
Thursday, 5-10 PM; Friday 5-11 PM; Saturday
6-11 PM
Reservations taken one week in advance for din-
ner; Call between 10:30-3 PM or 5-10 PM
Corkage: $5.00
Visa, MC

CHEF KEN HOM
P.O. Box 4303
Berkeley, CA 94704
No phone available
Not affiliated with a restaurant

HUNAN
924 Sansome St.
San Francisco, CA 94111
(415) 956-7727
853 Kearny St.
San Francisco, CA 94108
(415) 788-2234
Open Monday-Saturday, 11:30-9:30 PM
Reservations Accepted before 11 AM for lunch
and before 5 PM for dinner
Corkage: $5.00
Accommodation for private parties and group
dinners
MC, Visa, AX

KHAN TOKE
5937 Geary Blvd.
San Francisco, CA 94121
(415) 668-6654
Open 7 days a week; 5-11 PM
Reservations Accepted
Corkage: None permitted
AX, MC, Visa

KINOKAWA
347 Grant Ave.
San Francisco, CA 94108
(415) 956-6085
Open Monday-Friday, 11:30-2:30 PM;
Saturday-Sunday, 5-11 PM (Sushi bar open until
3 AM on Friday)
Reservations Recommended
Corkage: None permitted
Visa, MC, AX, DC, CB

KOREAN PALACE
631 O'Farrell St.
San Francisco, CA 94109
(415) 771-5353
Open Monday-Saturday, 11:30-2:30 PM, 5:30-
10 PM; Sunday, 5:30-9:30 PM
Reservations Accepted
Corkage: None permitted
Visa, MC, AX

MODESTO LANZONE'S
601 Van Ness Ave.-Opera Plaza
San Francisco, CA 94102
(415) 928-0400
900 North Point-Ghirardelli Square
San Francisco, CA 94109
(415) 771-2880
Opera Plaza: Open Monday-Friday 11 AM-12 PM,
Saturday 5 PM-1 AM
Ghirardelli: Open Tuesday-Friday 11:30 AM-
11 PM; Saturday-Sunday 4-12 PM
Reservations Required
Corkage: Upon Request
All major credit cards

APPENDIX
List of Restaurants: Pertinent Data

LEON'S BAR-BQ
1913 Fillmore St.
San Francisco, CA 94115
(415) 922-2436
2800 Sloat Blvd. (at 46th Ave.)
San Francisco, CA 94116
(415) 681-3071
Fillmore St.: Monday-Saturday, 11 AM-10 PM
Sloat Blvd.: Open 7 days; 11 AM-11 PM
Reservations Accepted but not required
Corkage: None permitted
Special catering for private parties
No credit cards

LIPIZZANER
2223 Union St.
San Francisco, CA 94123
(415) 921-3424
Open Tuesday-Saturday 5:30-10 PM
Reservations Recommended in advance
Corkage: $8.00
Visa, MC (no checks)

LITTLE JOE'S
523 Broadway
San Francisco, CA 94133
(415) 433-4343
Open 7 days a week; 11 AM-10:30 PM, except
Sunday, 1-9 PM
No reservations
Corkage: None permitted
No credit cards

MAMOUNIA
4411 Balboa St.
San Francisco, CA 94121
(415) 752-6566
200 Merrydale Road
San Rafael, CA 94903
(415) 472-1372
SF: Open Tuesday-Saturday 6-10 PM
San Rafael: Open Tuesday-Friday, 11-3 PM for
lunch; Tuesday-Saturday, 6-10 PM for dinner
Reservations Recommended
Corkage: None permitted
Visa, MC

THE MANDARIN
900 North Point-Ghirardelli Square
San Francisco, CA 94109
(415) 673-8812
Open 7 days a week; 12 Noon-11 PM
Reservations Recommended
Corkage: $4.50
Visa, MC, AX, DC, CB

MASA'S
648 Bush St.
San Francisco, CA 94108
(415) 989-7154
Open Tuesday-Saturday; First seating at 6 PM;
Last seating at 9 PM
Reservations 21 days in advance of date desired,
beginning at 10 AM that day
Corkage: $10.00
Visa, MC, AX

MAURICE ET CHARLES' BISTROT
901 Lincoln Ave.
San Rafael, CA 94901
(415) 456-2010
Open Monday-Saturday 6:30-10:30 PM
Reservations Recommended one week in
advance
Corkage: By request
Visa, MC, AX

MIFUNE
1737 Post St.
San Francisco, CA 94115
(415) 922-0337
Open 7 days a week; 11 AM-9 PM
No reservations accepted
Corkage: None permitted
Visa, MC, AX

MIRAMONTE
1327 Railroad Ave.
St. Helena, CA 94574
(707) 963-3970
Open Wednesday-Sunday, 6 PM on with last
seating at 9 PM
Reservations Recommended well in advance
Corkage: $8.00
Private rooms for parties 12-50
No credit cards

NARSAI'S
385 Colusa
Kensington, CA 94707
(415) 527-7900
Open Sunday-Thursday 5-10 PM; Friday-Saturday
5-11 PM
Reservations Recommended
Corkage: $5.00
Special regional dinners on Monday and Tues-
day nights, Beaujolais Festival in January, An-
niversary dinner in April, California Vintage
Festival in October
Visa, MC, AX, DC, CB

THE PEACOCK
2800 Van Ness Ave. (at Lombard)
San Francisco, CA 94109
(415) 928-7001
Open Sunday-Friday 11:30-2:30 PM, 5:30-10 PM;
Saturday 5:30-10 PM
Reservations Recommended
Corkage: $7.50
All major credit cards

THE RICE TABLE
1617 4th St.
San Rafael, Ca 94901
(415) 456-1808
Open Tuesday-Saturday, 5:30-10 PM; Sunday
5-9 PM
Reservations Recommended
Corkage: Not permitted
Visa, MC, AX, DC

APPENDIX
List of Restaurants: Pertinent Data

RISTORANTE DA LUCIANO
2018 Lombard
San Francisco, CA 94123
(415) 922-1900
Open Tuesday-Saturday 5-10:30 PM
Reservations Recommended
Corkage: $10.00
Visa, MC, AX

ROSE ET LE FAVOUR
1420 Main St.
St. Helena, CA 94574
(707) 963-1681
Open Wednesday-Saturday 6:30 PM-8:30 PM;
Sunday 1-3 PM
Reservations Required well in advance; Must
reconfirm 24 hours in advance
Corkage: $6 Wine; $8 Champagne & Sparkling
Wine
No credit cards

SCHROEDER'S
240 Front St.
San Francisco, CA 94111
(415) 421-4778
Open Monday-Friday, 11 AM-9 PM
Reservations Recommended but not required
Corkage: 50¢ per person
Mayfest (first 2 weeks of May), Oktoberfest (3rd
and 4th weeks of October)
AX

SQUARE ONE
190 Pacific (off Front)
San Francisco, CA 94111
(415) 788-1110
Open Monday-Friday 11:30-3 PM for lunch;
Monday-Saturday 5:30-11:30 PM for dinner
Reservations Recommended
Corkage: $7.00
Visa, MC

TADICH GRILL
240 California St.
San Francisco, CA 94111
(415) 391-2373
Open Monday-Saturday 11:30-8:30 PM
No Reservations
Corkage: $1.00 per person
No credit cards

TOMMASO'S
1042 Kearny St.
San Francisco, CA 94133
(415) 398-9696
Open Tuesday-Saturday 5-10:45 PM; Sunday
4-9:45 PM
No Reservations
Corkage: $5.00
Visa, MC

TON KIANG
5827 Geary Blvd.
San Francisco, CA 94121
(415) 387-8273

3148 Geary Blvd.
San Francisco, CA 94118
(415) 752-4440
683 Broadway
San Francisco, CA 94133
(415) 421-2015
Open 7 days a week; 11 AM-10:30 PM (Broadway
open until Midnight)
Reservations Accepted for 8 or more only
Corkage: None permitted
Visa, MC

RENÉ VERDON'S LE TRIANON
242 O'Farrell St.
San Francisco, CA 94102
(415) 982-9353
Open Monday-Saturday 6-10 PM
Reservations Recommended
Corkage: $12.00
Coats and ties required
All major credit cards

VIVANDE PORTA VIA
2125 Fillmore St.
San Francisco, CA 94115
(415) 346-4430
Open Monday-Friday 10 AM-7 PM; Saturday 10-6
PM; Sunday 10-5 PM; Cafe serves lunch daily
11:30-4 PM plus brunch starting at 10 AM on
Saturday and Sunday
No reservations
Corkage: $6.00
Special wine and food events, evening reserva-
tions for private parties, catering
Visa, MC, AX, DC, CB

XENIOS
2237 Polk St.
San Francisco, CA 94109
(415) 775-2800
Open 7 days a week; 10:30 AM-2 AM
Reservations Accepted
Corkage: $5.00
Special Easter dinner
All major credit cards

ZOLA'S
1722 Sacramento St.
San Francisco, CA 94109
(415) 775-3311
Open Tuesday-Sunday 6 PM-11 PM
Reservations Recommended
Corkage: $6.00 Wine; $10.00 Champagne
Regional dinners based on the food and wine
of specific regions of France
Visa, MC, AX

Code:
AC = American Express
MC = MasterCard
Visa = Visa
Diners or DC = Diners Club
CB = Carte Blanche

APPENDIX
List of Recipes by Course

PAGE

HORS D'OEUVRES

SOUPS & SALADS

MAIN COURSES
BEEF

VEAL

LAMB

PORK

APPENDIX
List of Restaurants/Chefs By Type of Cuisine

ABOUT THE AUTHOR

Sid Goldstein is a third generation native San Franciscan. He was born to a Jewish mother who wrote a cookbook herself when he was a teenager. This provided him with more than his share of gourmet treats at an early age and spoiled him forever.

In 1978, Goldstein wrote and produced *Napa Valley Wine Country*, a 16mm historical documentary film on the development and evolution of the Napa Valley as a winemaking region. The film has since become the standard reference on California winemaking.

In 1980, he found himself divorced after 11 years, wondering where his next good meal would be. Heroically, he plunged into the world of cooking for the first time and subsequently developed an original cookbook, *A Bachelor's Guide to Fine Food & Romance*, based on his research and experimentation. However, the title was made instantly obsolete by his own marriage and fatherhood.

The Spirit of Cooking is his first published book.